# Leafing through Literature

# Leafing through Literature

## Writers' Lives in Hertfordshire and Bedfordshire

David Carroll

The Book Castle

# For
# My Parents

First published July 1992
by the Book Castle
12 Church Street, Dunstable, Bedfordshire

© David Carroll

The right of David Carroll to be identified as Author of
this work has been asserted by him in accordance with
the Copyright, Designs and Patents Act 1988.

Computer typeset by 'Keyword', Aldbury, Hertfordshire
Printed and bound by Robert Hartnoll Ltd., Bodmin

ISBN 1 871199 01 8

# Contents

# Introduction

It is said that Shetland can boast more fiddlers per square mile than any other part of the British Isles. While the same may not be true about the density of writers in Hertfordshire and Bedfordshire, between them these two counties can certainly claim more than their fair share of literary associations.

Some of the authors included in this book – William Cowper and Graham Greene in Hertfordshire, for example; George Gascoigne and Mark Rutherford from Bedfordshire – were natives of the counties concerned. Others were drawn back over the years by family connections; Charles Lamb to Mackerye End, John Howard to Cardington.

With the development of the railways, from the middle of the nineteenth century, a number of famous writers settled in Hertfordshire or Bedfordshire, attracted by the opportunity to live deep in the country yet, at the same time, within easy reach of London. Both George Orwell at Wallington and Arnold Bennett at Hockliffe had this consideration in mind, as did Anthony Trollope when he moved to Waltham Cross.

Cycling – rather than driving – around the Hertfordshire lanes, during the course of many years, I constantly seemed to be coming across signposts with a literary flavour: Shaw's Corner at Ayot St. Lawrence, and Bulwer-Lytton's mansion at Knebworth. From George Chapman's more humble abode at Hitchin, it was but a short – and entirely logical – step to cross the border into neighbouring Bedfordshire. The next logical step, of course, was to write all about it.

No book which deliberately excludes living writers, can claim to be either exhaustive or definitive. Nevertheless, I hope that I have established most of the major – and many of the minor – literary connections which may be found in these two counties.

David Carroll
Beattock
November 1991

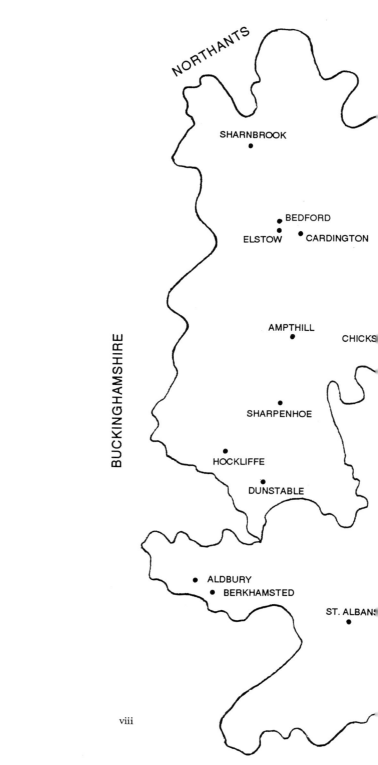

# A Literary Map of
## Hertfordshire & Bedfordshire

CAMBRIDGESHIRE

HAM

FFORD

BALDOCK

WALLINGTON

HITCHIN

STEVENAGE

KNEBWORTH

OT ST. LAWRENCE

WELWYN

WHEATHAMPSTEAD

LEMSFORD

WARE

HERTFORD

ESSENDON

HATFIELD

POTTERS BAR

WALTHAM CROSS

ESSEX

GREATER LONDON

# Author's Note

I have received help from many quarters during the preparation of this book, and I should like to thank all those people who have patiently answered my enquiries, and who were kind enough to supply me with photographs to illustrate the text. I owe a special debt to Eric Holland, who took photographs and made negatives of several subjects for me.

I am particularly grateful to Christine Hawkins, Assistant Librarian at the Hertfordshire Local Studies Collection, and Barry Stephenson, County Special Collections Librarian at Bedford, for their invaluable help in identifying useful research material, and for extending my horizons through their own local knowledge. This book would not have been possible, however, without the guidance and support of Paul Bowes; nor without the advice and encouragement of Bernadette Walsh, whose practical help at every turn made my task much easier.

# Graham Greene:

## Our Man from Berkhamsted

Graham Greene was fourteen when he knew that he must become a writer. 'I took Miss Marjorie Bowen's "The Viper of Milan" from the library shelf,' he recorded, 'and the future for better or worse really struck. From that moment I began to write. All other possible futures slid away; the potential civil servant, the don, the clerk had to look for other incarnations . . .'

Although it would be another eleven years before 'The Man Within', his first novel to be accepted, was published in 1929, Greene had been – by the time of his death in 1991 – one of Britain's most distinguished and consistently popular writers for sixty years. Many of his novels, including 'Brighton Rock', 'Our Man in Havana' and 'The Comedians' have become successful films – he also wrote 'The Third Man' for the cinema – and some have achieved the enduring status of twentieth-century classics. In addition to thirty or so novels, his prolific output included short stories, essays, travel books and plays.

For much of his long life, Graham Greene lived and worked abroad, and his extensive travels are reflected in some of his best fiction; 'The Honorary Consul' is set in Argentina, for example, and 'The Heart of the Matter' in West Africa. Less exotic, perhaps, but no less important to him, was Berkhamsted, where he was born in 1904. His father was Housemaster of St. John's at Berkhamsted School but later, in the autumn of 1910, Charles Greene succeeded Dr Fry as Headmaster, and the family moved to School House in Castle Street.

St. John's, in Chesham Road, was one of the boarding-houses of the school, with separate accommodation for the Master's family. When he was thirteen, Graham Greene would return – less happily – to St. John's as a boarder himself, while his family lived at School House. 'In those early days I had not even been aware that there existed in the same house such grim rooms as those I now lived in,' he wrote. 'I had left civilisation behind and entered a savage country of stange customs and inexplicable cruelties.'

*Berkhamsted School, where Graham Greene was a pupil. (Photo: Eric Holland.)*

The infant Greene, living at St. John's, had been much happier. One of his lasting memories from that time was of playing in the extra piece of garden belonging to the house but situated across the road from it. There, '. . . on special days in summer,' he recalled, 'we would go and play with the exciting sense of travelling abroad . . . Later I used to think of the two gardens as resembling England and France, with the Channel between – England for everyday and France for holidays.'

At School House, until he became a pupil himself just before his eighth birthday, Graham Greene's life revolved around the nursery, in what was really a conventional upbringing for an upper-middle-class child in the early years of this century. It was a large room, '. . . with toy-cupboards and bookshelves and a big wooden rocking-horse with wicked eyes.' This region was presided over by his nanny, whom he remembered with '. . . her head bent over his bath and her white hair in a bun.' Nevertheless, he also had two brothers and a couple of sisters with whom to share those early years.

There was, around this time, another branch of the Greenes – Charles Greene's brother, Edward, and his family – living in Berkhamsted, at The Hall, which was situated towards one end of the town. Graham Greene associated his uncle's house with Christmas Eve, in particular, when he would visit The Hall with his own family, to exchange presents and listen to carol-singing around the Christmas tree, 'afraid that I might be expected to sing too.'

Greene's cousin, 'Tooter', was his special friend, and sometimes they would sit together on the roof of The Hall, '. . . surveying the countryside, eating sweets . . . and planning their futures as midshipmen or Antarctic explorers.' This imposing house has since been demolished, to make room for the demands of modern housing.

Aunt Maud, Mrs Greene's unmarried sister, also lived in the town. Although she was generally regarded as something of a 'poor relation', she was also a 'walking newsletter', and it was partly this aspect of her character which appealed so strongly to her nephew. 'In later life I loved my aunt for this very quality,' he wrote, 'and would make journeys from London to have tea with her and hear the latest gossip of Berkhamsted. Her ear was very close to the ground.'

Despite the large number of his relatives who lived in Berkhamsted, (the family seemed 'to move as a tribe like the Bantus, taking possession,' he noted), Graham Greene was a shy boy, with a solitary nature; someone who enjoyed wandering about the town and surrounding countryside alone, perhaps already subconsciously storing up impressions for the time when he would one day become a writer.

The tow-path of the Grand Junction Canal, out of bounds to him as a very young child on afternoon walks with his 'crotchety old nurse', was a place of particular fascination as he grew slightly older, with its 'strange, brutal canal workers, [and] slow-moving painted barges.' Once, he befriended a couple of boys who lived in the town, and they met '. . . at the rubbish tips by the canal at the end of Castle Street,' to play cricket. He felt obliged to meet them in secret, however, because he was sure that his mother would not have approved of the liaison.

By the age of thirteen, Graham Greene had become increasingly unhappy at school; a situation he resolved – or, at least, partly ameliorated – by playing truant. It is possible that his rather ambiguous position as the Headmaster's son made life more difficult for him that it need have been. Berkhamsted Common, however, became his natural refuge on these occasions, where '. . . among the gorse and heather, and in the Ashridge beechwoods beyond,' he wrote, 'I could dramatize my loneliness and feel I was one of John Buchan's heroes, making his hidden way across the Scottish moors with every man's hand against him' In his late teens, during recurring periods of depression, he would go out beyond the Common and the grass ride known as Cold Harbour to Ashridge Park where, with live ammunition and his brother's revolver, he played Russian Roulette; a game he finally abandoned at Christmas 1923, and mercifully without having come to any harm.

Inevitably, for a born writer living very much in his imagination, the impressions and sensations that Graham Greene absorbed, and the personal memories associated with Berkhamsted from an early age have, to some extent, found their way into a number of his novels and short stories over the years. The town itself crops up in various guises; as Bishop's Hedron, for example, in the short story, 'The

Innocent', where 'in the autumn mist, the smell of wet leaves and canal water was deeply familiar.' However, in one of Greene's later novels, 'The Human Factor', published in 1978, Berkhamsted appears under its own name, and the local topography is drawn on extensively for the domestic life of the book's central character, Maurice Castle. He lives in King's Road and picnics on the Common with his family, where he shows his young stepson, Sam, 'the remnants of the old trenches dug in the heavy red clay during the first German war, by members of the Inns of Court O.T.C. . . .' Cycling to and from the station each day, he leaves his bicycle with the ticket-collector, whom he has known for years and, up on the London platform – one morning the train was forty minutes late because 'of repairs to the line somewhere beyond Tring' – he sees 'the cold October mist . . . lying in the grassy pool of the castle and dripping from the willows into the canal on the other side of the line.'

*Part of Berkhamsted Castle – a familiar landmark on Greene's 'personal map'.*

In the first volume of his autobiography, 'A Sort of Life', published in 1971, Greene described his birthplace – his 'personal map' as he called it – in great detail and revealed, in the process, some fascinating glimpses of a bygone Edwardian Berkhamsted. The old woman who lived in Castle Street, for example, and prepared tripe, ('a far lower occupation than a butcher's, though we frequently ate her tripe with white onion sauce'); old Mrs Figg's toy-shop, 'something like a crowded cabin,' in the High Street, 'where on bunk over bunk lay the long narrow boxes of Britain's toy soldiers . . .', and the afternoon when the whole family waited in the St. John's garden, 'on the English side of the road', hoping to see Bleriot making his flight from London to Manchester.

When Graham Greene left Berkhamsted in 1922, to become an undergraduate at Balliol College, Oxford, his Hertfordshire days were almost at an end, but his home-town exerted a certain influence on him which was not entirely erased by absence or old-age. 'For twenty years,' he wrote, 'it was to be almost the only scene of happiness, misery, first love, the attempt to write, and I feel it would be strange if, through the workings of coincidence, I was not brought back to die there in the place where everything was born.' In the event, however, he died – as indeed he had mostly lived – abroad, in hospital at Vevey in Switzerland.

# George Orwell:

# The Road to Wallington

Wallington, near Baldock, seems an unlikely place, perhaps, to find the author of 'Animal Farm' and 'Nineteen Eighty-Four' running a small general store; an improbable enough occupation in itself for a busy writer. When George Orwell moved to that small, north Hertfordshire village, however, during the spring of 1936, his two most famous novels were yet to be written. Although he had already published several books, and had been involved in journalism, his name was – as yet – known only to a relatively small band of followers.

George Orwell (whose real name was Eric Blair, and he was known as such in the village), moved into 'The Stores' in Kits Lane, after spending some time in the north of England, where he had been gathering material for the book which would become 'The Road to Wigan Pier'. He shared that not uncommon desire – and one that is now increasingly difficult to satisfy – for a quiet country retreat, which would afford him not only a peaceful environment in which to work, but would also provide a degree of self-sufficiency, with ideally a small piece of land on which to grow vegetables and keep a few animals. When some friends told Orwell about the empty cottage at Wallington, it sounded just the sort of thing he was looking for, and he decided to rent it – at 7/6d per week – without even looking over the property first.

Orwell arrived in Baldock – the nearest railway station to Wallington – on 2nd April and, as there was no 'bus service on that day to take him the three miles or so to the village, he made the rest of the way on foot. His life as a writer was not conducive to settling down in any one place for long; during the previous three years alone, for example, he had had six different homes. To a certain extent, 'The Stores' was to curb his wanderings, at least for a while. He lived in Wallington for probably longer than anywhere else during his adult life, and he certainly gave the impression to friends and acquaintances that he was happy there.

Orwell started life at Wallington as a bachelor but, just a few months later, on 9th June, he married Eileen O'Shaughnessy, whom he had known for just over a year. The ceremony, which was performed at the twelfth-century parish church of St. Mary's, was followed by a small reception for family and close friends at 'The Plough', a public-house situated just a few yards away from the Orwells' front door. George and Eileen had married without the safety-net of a secure, regular income. Orwell's most recent book, 'Keep the Aspidistra Flying', had been published a few weeks after he had moved to Wallington, but it had received a generally unenthusiastic reception, and he did not expect – or receive at that time – much in the way of an income from it. The need to supplement his rather erratic literary earnings spurred him on, no doubt, to re-open the general store, which had been kept by his predecessor at the cottage.

In making this decision, George and Eileen were conscious of the fact that whilst giving a much-needed boost to their own income, the shop should also be a welcome amenity in the village. They stocked up with a typically diverse range of goods but, alas, the project was not an outstanding success, and the takings were consistently and depressingly low. There was a 'bus service to Baldock several days a week where, with a wider choice of shops and probably lower prices, most of the villagers appeared to do their main shopping.

*The cottage (formerly 'The Stores') at Wallington, where Orwell wrote 'The Road to Wigan Pier'.*

*The Plough', Wallington: scene of the Orwells' wedding-reception in June 1936.*

The business operated from a small room at the front of the cottage, and Eileen calculated that the shop brought in on average less than three shillings a week. She usually attended to any customers, when she was at home but, in her absence, George would serve them, although this caused inevitable interruptions to his concentration when he was writing. The garden and livestock, however, proved to be less troublesome, (Orwell enjoyed getting up at 6.30am every day to milk the goats), and whatever produce they did not need themselves they were able to sell in the shop.

One of Wallington's greatest assets, so far as Orwell was concerned, was its inaccessibility coupled with its proximity to London; the same quality, in fact, that George Bernard Shaw was savouring about his life at that time over at Ayot St. Lawrence. Wallington – then, as now – was a small place; it had only one hundred or so inhabitants, and felt much more remote from the teeming capital than it actually was. Despite occasional – although necessary – interruptions from customers, Orwell was reasonably free from distractions at 'The Stores', where his major literary task during the summer of 1936 was writing 'The Road to Wigan Pier'. He was also regularly contributing articles to a variety of magazines.

The three-hundred year-old cottage was very basic, perhaps even primitive, when Orwell moved into it. There was no mains electricity and so oil-lamps were used for lighting. Calor gas provided the means of heating and cooking, and there was only cold running water. A privy at the end of the garden, and a corrugated-iron roof which, when it rained heavily, must have caused the Orwells to wonder if they were living in a tin-can, completed the picture of a rural idyll! To complicate matters further, Orwell was quite tall, and the oak-beamed ceilings were quite low with the inevitable result, according to visitors, that he was rarely able to stand upright inside the house.

A close friend, Elizaveta Fen, who visited the Orwells regularly during the four years they lived more-or-less full-time at 'The Stores', gives a neat impression of the austere nature of the place, in a memoir published in 'Twentieth Century', in August 1960. 'The weekends at the cottage were, in a sense, a test of endurance,' she wrote, '. . . The spare bedroom upstairs was as cold as an ice-box, even on June nights. Birds built their nests between the ceiling and the roof, and . . at night they would stamp and struggle overhead like an army of demons . . If one managed to stay asleep despite the cold and the birds, one would be awakened at half-past-six in the morning by the deafening peal of George's alarm-clock.' The redeeming feature after such a bad start to the day, it seems, was breakfast which almost invariably consisted of eggs from the Orwells' hens, bacon from a neighbour who kept pigs, and bread baked by Eileen.

The first six months of the Orwells' married life at Wallington coasted along on an even keel that might have remained undisturbed indefinitely had it not been for events abroad. In December, George decided that he had no alternative but to go to Spain and fight in the Civil War. He did so, leaving Eileen to cope alone at 'The Stores'. When he returned home – wounded – from the front, during the middle of 1937, their life resumed its old pattern until shortly after the outbreak of the Second World War. The intervening period was a productive one for Orwell. 'The Road to Wigan Pier' met with considerable success when it was published, in 1937, and it was followed, over the next three years, by 'Homage to Catalonia', resulting from his experiences in Spain; a novel, 'Coming Up for Air' and a volume of essays, 'Inside the Whale'. All four books were written largely at Wallington, punctuated by the serving of customers in the shop, milking goats, collecting eggs and sowing and tending vegetables in the garden.

Life at Wallington, on a full-time basis at least, ended for the Orwells in 1940, when Eileen started work for the Censorship Department in London. George stayed on alone at 'The Stores' for some time, and tried to keep things going until, as he hoped, they would both be back there together. Increasingly, however, he felt that he should be in London and, in any event, he was badly in need of a job with a regular income. Many of the periodicals to which he had been contributing had closed down at the outbreak of war.

As his Diaries reveal, Orwell often returned to Wallington for an odd day or two (and sometimes for longer), when his work at the B.B.C. and, later, as editor of 'The Tribune', allowed him to get away from London. (Poor health had disqualified him from military service.) 'At Wallington,' he recorded in a typical entry, dated March 4th 1941, 'crocuses out everywhere, a few wallflowers budding, snowdrops just at their best. Couples of hares sitting about in the winter wheat and gazing at one another. Now and again in this war, at intervals of months, you set your nose above water for a few moments and notice that the earth is still going round the sun.' It is impossible to believe that the Hertfordshire landscape and even his own livestock, did not play some part when he came to write 'Animal Farm', which appeared in 1945.

Eileen died – suddenly and quite unexpectedly – in 1945, but Orwell retained 'The Stores' as a weekend retreat for another year or so. In 1946, he moved to the Hebridean island of Jura, where he wrote his last book, 'Nineteen Eighty-Four'. He died from tuberculosis, in January 1950, at the age of forty-six.

# Sir Albert Richardson:

# 'The Complete Georgian' of Ampthill

The appearance of a sedan-chair on the streets of Ampthill during the inter-war years and later, must have caused some consternation in the hearts of many an onlooker, particularly if they were strangers to the area and happened to be unfamiliar with the engaging eccentricities of Professor Sir Albert Richardson, of Avenue House. Accompanied by volunteer porters in period costume and with a lantern-bearer leading the way, the vehicle – or 'parcel', as the Professor once memorably described it – must have led many bystanders to question their sobriety as its distinguished occupant, dressed in full eighteenth-century costume, was conveyed to a dinner engagement at a nearby house.

When Sir Albert Richardson died in February 1964, 'The Times' referred to him as 'the complete Georgian'. It was a description that he would no doubt have relished, capturing in an apt phrase his rather singular approach to life. As Simon Houfe wrote, in a lively account of his grandfather published in 1980, '. . . it was true that much he admired had ended in

1800, craftsmanship in the face of industry, pure classical architecture in the whirlpool of styles, a rural England in retreat from a metropolitan England.'

It was Avenue House, Ampthill – a handsome Georgian residence in a fine Georgian town – which provided the perfect ambience for Sir Albert to indulge his preference for all things eighteenth-century. He moved there – from St. Albans – during the summer of 1919, and it was to be his home for forty-five crowded years.

*Avenue House, Ampthill.*

Sir Albert – or the Professor, as he was always known – was an architect first and foremost; a profession to which, in one form or another, he was to devote the whole of his life. It was only a few months before his death, at the age of eighty-three, that he relinquished his last post – and one that was very dear to him – as Chairman of the H.M.S. Victory Technical Advisory Committee at Portsmouth. This was just one in a long line of appointments – for many years he was Bartlett Professor of Architecture at University College London and, subsequently, Professor of Architecture at the Royal Academy – which bore witness to the tremendously high regard in which his professional flair, knowledge and expertise were held, and which culminated in his two-year reign as President of the Royal Academy during the mid-1950s.

But the Professor was not only an architect par excellence: he was also a great communicator (a word, no doubt, that he would have deplored). If his hey-day had coincided with the golden age of television, then he would certainly have been courted by that medium. He was ideal material: not only a consummate expert in his field, blessed with the knowledge and enthusiasm to make his subject accessible to the layman, but he was also a true original in the honourable tradition of a Patrick Moore or David Bellamy.

Although the sheer bulk of the Professor's commitments meant that he was forever trying to squeeze a quart into a pint pot, he began writing quite early in his architectural career, initially publishing a number of essays on London's bridges and monuments in various evening newspapers. His first book, however, for which he had been researching and gathering material over a number of years, appeared in 1911, when he had just turned thirty. Written and illustrated in collaboration with Charles Lovett Gill, who was his business partner at that time, it was called 'London Houses from 1660 to 1820', and was a well-received anthology of the capital's Georgian streets and squares, packed with photographs and plans.

The success of this work led to an immediate commission from his publisher for the Professor's first single-handed effort. At a time when he was running a busy architectural practice of his own in conjunction with Gill, research for the new book involved him in long and sometimes arduous journeys to all parts of the British Isles and Ireland. The result, 'Monumental Classic Architecture in Great Britain and Ireland during the XVIIIth and XIXth Centuries', appeared in 1914, and became a standard work on the subject.

The Professor's first two books had been written while he was still living at St. Albans but, within a few years of moving to Ampthill, he completed a further three books in rapid succession. The first of these, 'Regional Architecture in the West of England' – another collaboration with Gill – owed its existence in large measure to the Professor's work as architect to the Duchy of Cornwall estates, and was published in 1924.

Hard on its heels came 'The Smaller English House of the Later Renaissance 1660–1830' – co-authored with an American writer, Harold Donaldson Eberlein – which, in its turn, was followed – in 1925 – by 'The English Inn Past and Present'. A revised version of this very successful book, re-titled 'The Old Inns of England', was issued ten years later. It was prefaced by Sir Edwin Lutyens and ran into a further five editions.

Perhaps the Professor's most popular book – one which had the widest appeal and in which he was able to draw freely on all the various strands of life from the period he delighted in – was 'Georgian England', published in 1930. It was an opportunity for him to share with his readers some of the material which he had accumulated over the years relating to the social life and arts and customs of the time, and it served as the ideal complement to his purely architectural works on the period.

Books, however – and there were more to follow, including 'The Art of Architecture' (1938), an 'Introduction to Georgian Architecture' (1946) and 'Robert Mylne : Architect and Engineer' (1956) – were only one aspect of the Professor's heavy writing schedule. As a comparatively young man in his thirties, he had been appointed editor of 'The Architectural Journal', and throughout his life he was a tireless contributor to many professional magazines and national publications, discoursing on every conceivable aspect of all things Georgian. He was also an occasional contributor to the 'Bedfordshire Magazine', until within a few years of his death; a valued link which had been established at the birth of that publication, when the Professor's article, 'Georgian Ampthill', appeared in the very first issue.

Although he was very much a national figure, the Professor was also one of that rare species: a prophet in his own home. Whatever the work that was occupying him elsewhere, nothing prevented him from taking a minute interest in developments close at hand. A glance at just a few of his responsibilities, at an age when most men would have been retired – standing member of the Royal Fine Arts Commission, council member of the Georgian Group, adviser to the dioceses of Ely, St. Albans and Southwark, and architect to the fabric of York Minster; not to mention his permanent courses of university lectures, lecture tours around the country and his own busy practice – gives some indication of the endless calls on his time. It had been ever thus, and yet he still managed to be a conspicuous force in the life of Ampthill.

Perhaps two local projects in particular neatly demonstrate the wide range of the Professor's interests. During the 1920s, he was instrumental in organizing a lengthy – but ultimately successful – campaign to save the ruins of Houghton House. The decaying property, linked with Bunyan's 'House Beautiful' of 'The Pilgrim's Progress', had been a source both of interest and regret to him during his walks from Avenue House. The remains, however, were still of considerable architectural significance, and the Professor was understandably delighted to have won the day.

*The remains of Houghton House.*

Two decades later found him with a request from Ampthill Rural District Council, to create a model housing scheme on the edge of town. With no less enthusiasm and gusto than he would have applied to any of his more famous projects, the Professor embarked on creating what he described as '£1 a week mansions', set on a three-acre site around a village green.

The 1950s proved to be a decade of crowning glory for the Professor. By now into his seventies, these were the years which saw his election as President of the Royal Academy and the award of his knighthood. At home in Bedfordshire, however, he became embroiled in a controversy which caught the public imagination. It concerned the placing of thirty-foot high concrete lamp-posts, or 'concrete attenuated penguins', as he described them, in the Georgian streets of Ampthill. Sadly, he was defeated on his home ground, after spending so much of his life advising Local Authorities the length and breadth of the land on the sensitive blending of things ancient and modern.

During the last twenty years or so of his life, the Professor kept a journal of – it has been suggested – almost Pepysian proportions, in which he meticulously recorded everyday appointments and activities, his views on life and the world around him. He moved in influential – and sometimes exalted – circles and, should they ever be edited and published, his diaries would no doubt give a picture every bit as spontaneous and detailed as the tiny watercolours he was so fond of executing (often using improvised materials) to illustrate a point or for the simple enjoyment of friends. An intimate and idiosyncratic account of mid-twentieth century England from the pen of 'the complete Georgian', would provide a fascinating literary postscript to the life and work of Professor Sir Albert Richardson, of Ampthill.

*St. Andrew's church, and a quiet Georgian corner of Ampthill.*

# A Picture of Innocence:

# E M Forster at Stevenage

E M Forster was not a prolific novelist by most standards; he wrote only six and the last, 'A Passage to India', appeared in 1924, almost half a century before his death. During the last forty-six years of his life he produced short stories, essays, criticism and biographies but, with the exception of 'Maurice', completed in 1914 and published posthumously in 1971, there were to be no more novels. If Forster's output of fiction during his long life lacked quantity, then the quality and enduring appeal of his work is beyond question. His novels are not only widely read but, in recent years, most of them have been filmed, sometimes with outstanding success; reaffirming his status as one of the twentieth century's most important writers.

Literary success, however, was very much a thing of the future when four year-old Forster arrived at Rooksnest, Stevenage, in March 1883. His mother had been recently widowed and decided to leave Bournemouth, where she had moved a few years earlier for the sake of her husband's health.

Rooksnest was the successful conclusion to a protracted period of house-hunting. 'I should not have chosen to live in such a lonely place,' she wrote to a friend, 'but I can't find anything else and here is winter upon me again.'

At that time, of course, during the late nineteenth century, Stevenage was no more than a village and a very different place to the large town that exists today. Rooksnest was set on its own, a mile or so along the road to Weston. When he was older – and after he had moved away from Hertfordshire, in 1893 – Forster wrote about the house and its surroundings with deep affection; a sentiment he was to retain for the place throughout his life. Arriving by train from London on the Great Northern Railway he recalled that, during the journey, he had pronounced 'Welwyn', one of the stations along the route, '. . . as it is spelt and not as 'Wellin', in the approved fashion.' The view from the house itself, he declared, was a revelation to 'people who were accustomed to call Herts. an ugly county . . .'

The rent for this substantial house, with four acres attached, was £55 per year and, despite Mrs Forster's reservations about its isolated position, (a consideration that would not arise in the same way today), she recognized that there was much to recommend it as a home, not least 'the good sanitary arrangements', with which she expressed herself well satisfied. Forster, however, seemed to view them in a different light. In his essay about Rooksnest, he complains that they lived without running water for about six years, and that they were obliged to draw off what they needed from a well on the farm. Their daily quota of two bucketsful – for which, said Forster, they paid 'a fabulous price' – was supplemented by rainwater which, presumably, was trapped in a water-butt. Later, however, their landlord, Colonel Wilkinson, arranged for a small waterworks to be built nearby, and this made the Forsters' lives much easier – except during the winter when the pipes froze!

E M Forster adored Rooksnest. The house, neighbours, the locality itself, were all a source of endless pleasure and fascination to him. Given his comparatively small output of fiction, they were to make a significant contribution to his writing later on. For most of the time mother and son comprised the household, but Forster's grandmother and a great-aunt were frequent visitors. In the absence of his father, the young boy was almost exclusively surrounded by women; a situation of which his grandmother did not entirely approve, so she formed with him 'an alliance . . . against all old cats of women, with their gossip and sewing-parties.'

Aware of her son's need for companions nearer to his own age, however, Mrs Forster employed a number of local lads over the years to work in the garden at Rooksnest. Usually they performed a dual role: tending lawns and flower-beds during working-hours, and playing with the son of the house when they were off duty. Some of these boys were among Forster's earliest friends and one youngster, Ansell, 'a snub-nosed, pallid, even-tempered youth,' became the eponymous hero of a tale that Forster wrote at the turn of the century, (although it was not published until 1970). The story recalls how the narrator (the spirit of young Forster himself?) and a garden-boy at 'The Hall', '. . . scraped out a hole in the side of a large straw stack, and made it into a house where we stored apples and gooseberries, and "Kola" lemonade, which we got cheap from Ansell's aunt in the village.' Forster shared with Ansell many experiences similar to those he described in the short story. The real-life Ansell '. . . built a straw pent-house' in the Rooksnest garden, which he and Forster used as a den and an apple store.

Among the Forsters' immediate farming neighbours were a family called Franklyn, who rented a meadow from the Rooksnest tenant. Towards the end of his life, Forster was pleased to recall that, over the years, he had known five generations of them. One of his companions was young Frankie, Mr Franklyn's grandson, and the two boys would play endlessly together around the farm and its outbuildings. There were barns and stables to be explored, of course, and always eggs to be collected. Frankie was by far the more adventurous of the two boys. It was he who would play on the old farmyard machinery while Forster, it seems, could only look on enviously.

The influence that Rooksnest exerted on Forster was so potent that it was almost inevitable, from the moment he became a writer, the house would find its way into one of his novels or short stories. For 'Howards End', published in 1910,

Forster drew not only on the house itself but also upon some of the people he had known during that part of his life, in Hertfordshire. More than one local family of his acquaintance might have been the prototype for the Wilcoxes, who are the central characters in his book. 'The garden, the overhanging wych-elm, the sloping meadow, the great view to the west . . ' he wrote, 'were all utilized by me in "Howards End".' Strangely, although Forster was not aware of it until much later, the house had at one time been called 'Howards', and named after the family who had owned it at an earlier date.

*Rooksnest, Stevenage: the original of 'Howards End'. (Copyright: Margaret Ashby).*

The Forsters left Rooksnest in 1893. In the first place their lease, which had already been extended several times beyond its original three years, had expired and Colonel Wilkinson was unable to renew it again. Secondly, Forster was due to start school at Tonbridge and, presumably, his mother thought it desirable to be close at hand. From the moment that he moved away from the house, however, Forster never ceased to regard the years he had spent at Rooksnest as an idyllic chapter in his life.

In 1906, when he had left university, and was living with his mother at Abinger Hammer, in Surrey, Forster returned to

Stevenage on a brief visit. He called on the Franklyns, of course and, now that he had grown into a young gentleman, was much honoured by having tea in their best parlour. When he was a young child living at Rooksnest, no doubt it was a room from which he had been excluded at all costs! Afterwards, he went off with Frankie to explore all their old haunts around the farm.

Many years later, when he was in search of a permanent home at the end of the Second World War, Forster actively considered returning to the Stevenage area, with all its happy childhood associations; memories made all the more golden, perhaps, by the passing of time. He was disappointed, however, to find that the village once so dear to him, was about to be engulfed by the twentieth century. It was scheduled for redevelopment as a 'new town' with an estimated influx of 60,000 people, and he decided against moving back there.

In the event, Forster lived for much of the rest of his life in a set of rooms at King's College, Cambridge, where he was elected to an Honorary Fellowship in 1946. Even here, however, there was a tangible reminder of his Hertfordshire days. It appears that, when Mrs Forster finally left Rooksnest, she had been allowed to take with her a favourite mantlepiece, which had then been transferred to each of Forster's successive homes; until it finally arrived in his rooms at King's College where, he declared, it looked 'more effective than ever.'

In 1956, Forster published a biography of his great-aunt, called 'Marianne Thornton', in which he described Rooksnest as 'a lovable little house . . . though it now stands just outside a 20th-century hub and almost within sound of a 20th-century hum.' While he was not altogether at ease with its new surroundings: more houses, more roads and the miscellaneous clutter of modern technology, the house itself retained a magic for him. In a diary entry made in 1944, written more than fifty years after leaving the place, he could still describe Rooksnest as '. . . my childhood and my safety.'

# The Man from the North:

## Arnold Bennett at Hockliffe

The twin peaks which have ensured Arnold Bennett's reputation as a major twentieth-century novelist are undoubtedly 'The Old Wives' Tale' and 'Clayhanger', both of which are set in the Potteries; that part of Staffordshire where Bennett was born and spent the first twenty years of his life. Other novels, including 'Anna of the Five Towns', 'These Twain' and 'Hilda Lessways', together with countless short stories, have their origins in the same area, and Arnold Bennett has become synonymous with that northern region of clay and kilns.

What, then, were the circumstances which led Bennett to the small south Bedfordshire village of Hockliffe, straddling Watling Street, at the turn of the century? It was not an obvious move – even given his half-hearted resolve to live in the country – for a single man in his early thirties who had spent more than a decade in London where, through grim determination to succeed in the literary world, he had risen from being a humble clerk in a legal firm to the editorship of

'Woman' magazine. Furthermore, amongst his large and diverse output of articles, plays, serials and short stories, his first novel, 'A Man from the North', had appeared in 1898. If he was not yet quite so famous as he one day would be, then London seemed the obvious place to improve on his growing success.

Bennett's desire to live in the country – perhaps originally conceived as a solution to constantly overworking in London – was fuelled by the realization that many of his most eminent contemporaries, including Hardy, Kipling and Henry James, had opted for a predominantly rural life. When his father, Enoch, became seriously ill, and was advised to leave the Potteries, Bennett's vague intention became at once a fixed plan. After resigning his editorship of 'Woman' in September 1900, 'I reached down a map of England,' he explained, 'and said that I must live on a certain main-line at a certain maximum distance from London.' Thus it was, by that slightly random method, Bennett arrived at the beginning of the following month with his parents and his sister, Tertia, to take up residence at Trinity Hall Farm, Hockliffe.

Bennett arranged to lease the property, which was owned by John James Reynal Adams, a member of an old Bedfordshire family, through the Leighton Buzzard surveyor, A W Merry. The outward appearance of the house was unremarkable, but Bennett enjoyed the novelty of living at the end of a drive which led directly off Watling Street. 'After all,' he declared, 'few people can stamp the top of their notepaper "Watling Street, England"!'

Within a few weeks, Arnold Bennett had settled sufficiently well into his new home, to be able to write enthusiastically to friends in London; many of whom, knowing how much he relished metropolitan life, had been openly sceptical about his proposal to leave town. 'The scenery . . is very Great, and Great are the villages,' he told John Rickard. 'Greatest of all is Watling Street sweeping past my meadow . . in a tremendous straight line . . I should mention,' he added, 'that this place is set on a hill, with a clear view of miles of downs – amid Bunyan's "Delectable Mountains".'

The rural life clearly suited Arnold Bennett. The countryside around Hockliffe offered so many delights that were new to a man who had spent all his life either in the industrial landscape of the Potteries or in London. Early January 1901 finds him waxing lyrical in his Journal, about two ploughing teams he had recently seen working in a nearby field: their '. . . large, slow, dignified movements . . as picturesque as that of vessels coming into harbour early on a misty morning. I think that never before,' he wrote, 'have I regarded a land-movement as being equal in picturesqueness to a sea-movement.' That was praise indeed from a man who loved boats and the water. 'I shall never have a study more ideally placed than this,' he told his friend, the Surrey writer, George Sturt, 'not even by the sea.'

For Arnold Bennett, Hockliffe actually represented the first major step in a long-term plan, '. . . towards that country mansion which I am going to build (before I am forty), by the sea's margin.' But Trinity Hall Farm also provided him – in theory at least – with a breathing-space; a peaceful environment in which to take stock of his position. For Bennett was, above all, an industrious man, prepared to turn his hand to most aspects of his trade.

Magazine editor and working journalist, playwright, novelist, reviewer and publisher's reader; Bennett was all these things, and some of the roles overlapped for much of the 1890s. Financially, at least, and as the means of securing his true independence, Bennett felt that his future lay in writing novels. 'To write popular fiction is offensive to me,' he said, 'but it is far more agreeable than being tied daily to an office and editing a lady's[sic] paper.'

'A Man from the North' was Bennett's only novel prior to the Hockliffe years, although he had also written a 70,000 word serial which would later appear in book form as 'The Grand Babylon Hotel'. From the turn of the century, however, novels were to become an increasingly important feature of his still varied output. Some of these were better received than others over the next thirty years but, with the publication of 'The Old Wives' Tale' in 1908 and 'Clayhanger' two years later, he ceased to be merely a well-known man of letters, and became one of the most celebrated writers of his period.

Arnold Bennett's tendency to write novels of variable quality was well illustrated during the few years he lived in

Bedfordshire. When he arrived at Trinity Hall Farm Bennett was already at work on a novel which he had provisionally entitled 'Anna Tellwright'. He finished it on 17th May 1901, at 2.45am, to be exact, after which he '. . . slept well for 4 hours, got up with a frightful headache, and cycled through Hemel Hempstead to St. Albans, lunched at "The George", and home – 42 miles!' The novel was published during the following year as 'Anna of the Five Towns'. It is generally regarded as one of his finest books, and has become a twentieth-century classic.

Another novel from the same period, however, shows Bennett working in a different key. 'Teresa of Watling Street', long forgotten and out-of-print until it was re-issued in 1989, was Bennett's one attempt at detective fiction. In other circumstances, it would hardly merit particular attention – indeed, the author himself is reported to have been slightly embarrassed when it was given a new lease of life as a book in 1904, after it had first appeared as a serial – but it has a special connection with his Bedfordshire days. Much of the plot is centred around the village of Hockliffe; and Trinity Hall Farm, called Queen's Farm in the novel, becomes the home of a mysterious London banker, Raphael Craig, and his daughter, the eponymous Teresa, two of the book's main characters.

*Trinity Hall Farm, Hockliffe: the setting for 'Teresa of Watling Street'. (Photo: by kind permission of Simon Houfe.)*

27

Bennett's topography is detailed and accurate, suggesting that he developed more than just a passing interest in the village which, for a while at least, became his home. He deftly captures, in more than one passage, the period charm of early twentieth-century Hockliffe. 'The steam plough rattled and jarred and jolted like a humorous and high-spirited leviathan,' he wrote. 'The Chiltern Hills stretched away in the far distance, bathed in limitless glad sunshine; and Watling Street ran white, dazzling and serene, down the near slope and up the hill towards Dunstable, curtained in the dust of rural traffic.'

Local interest in the story hinges not only upon the sense of place, but on some of the village characters that Bennett drew, as well. Pre-eminent among these is Mr Puddephatt, 'a large, stout man dressed in faded grey, with a red, cheerful face and an air of unostentatious prosperity.' He is the village wine-merchant, and the native voice of Hockliffe. Speculation over the years, concerning whether or not Puddephatt was a portrayal of a specific individual known to Bennett locally or an amalgam of several people, has linked the character with Arthur J Willison, the Hockliffe tailor who, in Arnold Bennett's day, lived at the house ascribed to Puddephatt in the story, '. . . the first dwelling in the village . . . as you enter it by Watling Street . . . a small double-fronted house with a small stable at the side thereof.' Willison and Bennett were certainly well acquainted and the former, like Mr Puddephatt, also dealt in horses and was an inexhaustible fund of village lore and history.

Realistically, life at Hockliffe was never destined to be much more than a pleasant interlude for Arnold Bennett. A filial concern for his dying father had, in the end, been the driving force behind his move to the village, and for setting up home under the same roof as his parents and sister. When Enoch Bennett died, therefore, in January 1902, his death signalled the end of the family's connection with the area. Mrs Bennett – after her husband's burial at nearby Chalgrave – returned to the Potteries and, a year or so later, Arnold Bennett gave up Trinity Hall Farm altogether, having visited it only occasionally in the meantime. He went off to France, where he was to live for the next ten years.

Later, in middle-age, Arnold Bennett was to acquire that

'country mansion . . by the sea's margin', at Thorpe-le-Soken on the Essex coast, but London claimed him in the end, just as his friends knew that it would. 'Teresa of Watling Street', however, for all its possible imperfections is, nevertheless, a permanent reminder of one famous author's sojourn in Bedfordshire.

*Enoch Bennett's*
*tombstone at Chalgrave.*

# Nursery Tales:

## Beatrix Potter at Camfield Place

The low hills of Furness, in the southern Lake District, were Beatrix Potter's country and, in particular, the village of Near Sawrey, set between Grizedale Forest and the western shores of Windermere. She had known the area since childhood, accompanying her parents there, well into her own middle-age, on their long summer holidays. It was the part of the world from which she drew inspiration for many of her children's stories and the illustrations which complemented them, and she described Near Sawrey, where eventually she owned Hill Top Farm and a great deal more property, as 'nearly perfect a place as I ever lived in.' She spent the last thirty years of her life there, at Castle Cottage, as Mrs William Heelis, a highly respected sheep-farmer and the wife of a country solicitor.

As a child, however, and until well into her twenties, Beatrix Potter was deeply attached to Camfield Place at Essendon, near Hatfield; a house which in more recent years has been the home of the writer, Dame Barbara Cartland. Grandfather Potter and his wife bought the property, which included a three-hundred acre estate, in 1866, to live in during their retirement. Having spent their working lives in the Lancashire cotton industry, where they had made and lost a fortune before accumulating another one, Mr and Mrs Edmund Potter moved south possibly to be nearer their grandchildren, or simply to reap the benefits of a less hostile climate in old-age.

Beatrix Potter was born in the same year that her grandparents acquired Camfield Place, and so it formed a cornerstone of her early life. Given its proximity to London, where she lived in South Kensington with her parents, Beatrix was a frequent visitor to the house for more than twenty years. In 1891, when both of her grandparents were dead and her association with the house was almost at an end, she wrote of it as 'my Blakesmoor', echoing the sentiments that Charles Lamb had expressed in his essays for Blakesware, near Widford.

When Beatrix Potter was fifteen, she began to keep a secret journal, written in an elaborate code of her own invention. Over a period of sixteen years or so, from 1881 to 1897, she recorded both the important events and the minutiae of her daily life. Her descriptions of the people with whom she came into contact mainly through her parents, – including Sir John Millais, the artist, and Gladstone – and of the places she visited, are not only a delight to read in themselves, but they are also an invaluable account of upper-middle-class life during the late Victorian era.

It was only at the beginning of the 1950s, that parts of the journal first came to light, buried away in a drawer at Castle Cottage. Even so, it was to be several years later – in 1958 – that Leslie Linder actually deciphered the code. Years of exhaustive transcription work followed until, in 1966, he was able to publish 'The Journal of Beatrix Potter', to coincide with the centenary of her birth.

The journal, of course, makes many references to Camfield Place, and to Beatrix Potter's feelings for the house and the memories associated with it. She recalled in her mid-twenties that, as a very young child, of perhaps only two years old, she had lain in '. . . a crib in the nursery bedroom, under the tyranny of a cross old nurse . . I can feel the diamond pattern of that old yellow crib printed against my cheek,' she wrote, 'as I lay with my head where my heels should be.' The clarity of that early memory, so fondly recalled many years later, is testimony to her love for Camfield Place, where she was awoken '. . . on summer mornings by the persistent crying of a cuckoo . . . I believe the record was fifty-two cries before seven o'clock, till tired of counting.'

*Camfield Place, Essendon. (Photo: by kind permission of Dame Barbara Cartland.)*

Perhaps Beatrix Potter's affection for her grandparents' house was amplified, to some extent, by the marked contrast it provided with her own home in Kensington, which was rather dark and sombre. Life at Bolton Gardens ran on well-oiled lines, and to an inflexible, punctually-observed timetable. For a less self-sufficient child, or for one whose inner life was not so well-developed as Beatrix Potter's, long, solitary days in the nursery on the third floor might have been unbearably lonely. Instead, they gave her the opportunity to read avidly, and to develop the imagination that would one day serve her so well as a writer and artist.

Edmund Potter, Beatrix's grandfather, died in 1883, and so it is of her grandmother, who lived until 1891, that the clearest – and perhaps fondest – picture emerges. There seems to have been a special rapport between Mrs Edmund Potter and her granddaughter, and Beatrix recalled that, as a child, she would sit beneath the library table at Camfield Place, listening to the old lady's conversation, while eagerly consuming '. . . the hard gingersnap biscuits which her grandmother gave her privately from a canister, and on which, one by one, [Beatrix] loosened her milk teeth.'

Beatrix Potter's early years were marked by a scarcely less fervent passion for the undramatic, wooded landscape of Hertfordshire, than she was to experience later for the rugged Lakeland fells. Writing in 1884, she reported the general feeling of the time, that another fifty years or so would bring London out to Hatfield. A cursory glance at any recent Ordnance Survey map of the area, will tell its own story, and while she would still find much to admire around Camfield Place today – only a few miles yet, in its peaceful seclusion, light-years away from Hatfield and Welwyn Garden City – she would find that much had altered, too, over the last one hundred years.

Such changes, however, were very much in the future when Beatrix Potter was a visitor to Camfield Place. 'If you get on any rising ground in this neighbourhood,' she recorded, 'you would fancy Hertfordshire was one great oak wood.' citing as an example a striking autumnal view from Essendon Hill. The area is still rich in woodland today; even if it is a trifle fragmented, and bisected by many more roads than Beatrix Potter would have thought possible.

It is strange, perhaps, given her attachment to the area, that neither Camfield Place nor Hertfordshire in general emerges very distinctly – indeed, hardly at all – in Beatrix Potter's stories and illustrations. Visits to her cousin, Caroline Hutton, who lived at Harescombe Grange near Stroud, provided the impetus for 'The Tailor and Gloucester' and, to a lesser extent, 'The Tale of Two Bad Mice'; while holidays in the West Country gave her the idea for 'The Tale of Little Pig Robinson'. Most of her books, however, owed their origins in one way or another to the Lake District.

Beatrix Potter did suggest, so far as Mr McGregor's garden is concerned, in 'The Tale of Peter Rabbit', that 'the potting-shed and the actual geraniums were in Hertfordshire.' She didn't specify Camfield Place, so perhaps it might have been Bush Hall or Woodfield, two country houses not far from Essendon and Hatfield, where Beatrix and her parents spent their summer holidays in 1883 and 1884.

Camfield Place, however, is definitely associated with 'Cecily Parsley's Nursery Rhymes', a collection which finally appeared in 1922. The last ryhme in the book:

'Ninny Nanny Netticoat
In a white petticoat
With a red nose –
The longer she stands
The shorter she grows,'

is illustrated by a group of mice taking tea around a lighted candle, and recalls 'the cross old nurse' in the nursery bedroom. Beatrix, and her young cousins who sometimes stayed at Camfield Place, called the nurse 'Nanny Netticoat', and her appearance reminded the children of a candle.

Beatrix Potter's journey from London and Hertfordshire, to her eventual home in the Lake District, was a much greater leap than the mere geographical distance or number of intervening years would suggest. It was a hard, uphill struggle for her, both psychologically and in practical terms, as a single woman – a dutiful daughter who, until her late marriage, never questioned her parents' authority – to emerge from the sheltered background in which she had been brought up, to become a sheep farmer and breeder, and the wife of a solicitor practising at Hawkshead. That she accomplished it at all, and that the last thirty years of her life, at Castle Cottage, Near Sawrey, were her happiest and most satisfying, is some indication of the strength of character which lurked behind her quiet demeanour.

Beatrix Potter was pleased to forget London, and consign it to her past, but Hertfordshire was another matter. Margaret Lane, in her biography, 'The Tale of Beatrix Potter', draws a cosy picture of Beatrix and William Heelis alone in their cottage and, in the long, dark winter evenings, poring over – as they were wont to do – 'those curious cipher manuscripts [Beatrix's journal], written "long ago and in another world", when she had sat drawing butterflies at the library table at Camfield Place, her eyes on her book and her whole spirit drinking in her grandmother.'

# J M Barrie:

# Peter Pan at Berkhamsted

For three years 'Peter Pan', 'the little boy who would not grow up' lived, not among the fairies in Kensington Gardens, as J M Barrie would want us to believe but, rather more prosaically, at Egerton House, Berkhamsted. It was towards the end of 1904 that Arthur Llewelyn Davies, his wife Sylvia and their five sons – most, if not all, of whom made some contribution to the immortal character – moved from their existing home at Kensington Park Gardens, to the small Hertfordshire town once much-beloved of the Black Prince and where, in 1389, Chaucer was appointed Clerk of Works at the Castle. (It was an office which he held only for a couple of years, and for much of that time a deputy officiated in his place, while Chaucer pursued other interests elsewhere.)

Neither the town's connections with the Black Prince nor with the author of 'The Canterbury Tales', it must be said, were Berkhamsted's primary attractions for Arthur Llewelyn Davies. He was more interested in the fact that the house was close to a railway station and that the town, although tucked away in the country, was within easy commuting distance of London. (Arthur was a barrister, and he travelled up to his chambers at the Temple every day.) Egerton House was also larger than the Davies's previous home – an essential consideration for a growing family – and it had, by all accounts, a most attractive garden. The fact that Berkhamsted School was just a few minutes' walk from the house and, with its superb reputation, ideally placed for educating at least some of Arthur's five sons, completed the list of inducements.

*Egerton House, Berkhamsted, at the beginning of this century. (Photo: Berkhamsted & District Local History Society.)*

It was in Kensington Gardens, of course, where the 'Peter Pan' statue serves as a permanent reminder of the occasion that, sometime during 1897, J M Barrie – already a famous author and playwright – met the two little boys, in the company of their nurse, who were to inspire the creation of what is probably his most enduring character. George, then aged five and his brother, Jack, aged four, were the first of the Davies boys to make Barrie's acquaintance. It was initially for their enjoyment alone the story was concocted that would later, at Christmas 1904, take to the stage with such success as 'Peter Pan'.

'What was it,' wrote Barrie somewhat wistfully, in 1928, 'that made us eventually give to the public in the thin form of a play that which had been woven for ourselves alone?' Barrie always maintained that the character of Peter was actually a composite of several – and possibly all five – of the Davies boys. 'I made Peter by rubbing the five of you violently together,' he said, 'as savages with two sticks produce a flame.' And surely it must have been the case, as Barrie came to know the whole family after meeting the boys' mother quite by chance at a dinner-party, that Peter, Michael and Nicholas played their part, too.

Life at Egerton House augured well for Arthur and Sylvia. They were devoted to each other, and had five happy, healthy sons. Also Arthur was gradually becoming more prosperous. 'They have a beautiful Elizabethan house,' wrote Dolly Ponsonby, a family friend, after a visit to Berkhamsted early in 1905. 'Nothing could be more perfect than the inside, especially for so large a family. There are huge nurseries and a school-room with mullioned windows . . odd-shaped bedrooms with beams and sloping floors – and all so charmingly done . . . with harmonious chintzes and lovely bits of Chippendale furniture.' Peter Llewelyn Davies was to describe it later as 'a gracious, happy, pretty, comfortable home.'

The house at Berkhamsted was distinguished by its informal atmosphere. Neither Sylvia nor Arthur, by all accounts, were typical parents in the Edwardian sense, and their relationships with the five boys were decidedly relaxed. 'Arthur,' wrote Dolly Ponsonby, 'was so tender and gentle with children, that I never met one who feared him.' J M Barrie, writing about Mr and Mrs Darling and their children in 'Peter Pan', said that 'there never was a simpler, happier family . . .', but he was really describing the Llewelyn Davieses. To some extent, Arthur was caricatured as Mr Darling in the play.

'Peter Pan' opened at the Duke of York's theatre, in London, on 27th December 1904. Earlier in the month, Sylvia had taken her sons up to town to visit rehearsals, whereupon Barrie informed the cast that it was really the Davies boys who had written the play or, at least, there would have been no 'Peter Pan' without them. Immediately after Christmas, the boys attended the play's first matinée; an occasion that was followed by tea at Barrie's home.

The following Christmas – setting a pattern which has continued up to the present day – 'Peter Pan' was again staged in London, but Michael Llewelyn Davies, then aged five, was ill and could not go to the theatre to see it. Determined that one of the play's creators should not miss out on the event, Barrie transported the scenery and the whole cast of the play up to Berkhamsted, where a 'command performance' of 'Peter Pan' was given for Michael in his nursery at Egerton House, on 20th February 1906. Barrie went to great lengths to have a special programme printed for the occasion, and he also took a small part in the performance; the only time he ever appeared in one of his own plays.

While 'Peter Pan' went from strength to strength in Britain and abroad, ensuring literary immortality for its author, the Davies boys lived – if not exactly quietly, then certainly very happily – at Berkhamsted where, by the spring of 1905, they had become fully adjusted to country life. Such happiness, however, was destined not to last.

During the first few months of 1906, Arthur became ill with cancer. After undergoing surgery at a London nursing home in June, however, he was able to return to Egerton House. 'Here is my last letter of all before coming home to Berkhamsted and my boys,' he wrote to Michael, on 27th June. 'We are coming all the way in Mr Barrie's motor-car. After tea tomorrow, you will take me carefully for a walk all round the garden, and show me all the flowers that have come up since we went away.' (Sylvia had stayed in London to be near him.)

Throughout the next couple of months, Arthur seemed to be making excellent progress but, in September, he suffered a recurrence of his earlier symptoms. He now had to brace himself – and Sylvia – for the prospect that he would not recover nor, in fact, live very much longer.

Thus so swiftly did the great happiness of life at Egerton House turn to deep sorrow. Despite overwhelming demands on his time Barrie, true to character, was a great support to the Llewelyn Davieses during Arthur's illness, and he spent as much time at Berkhamsted as his busy timetable would allow. His elegant Lanchester motor-car and distinguished-looking chauffeur became a familiar sight in the area for a while. By

the spring of 1907, however, Arthur was unable to speak, and
he died on 18th April.

*Berkhamsted High Street, 1991. Egerton House was
demolished in 1937, but Egerton Terrace can be glimpsed
on the left. (Photo: Eric Holland.)*

There was no question of Sylvia living indefinitely at Egerton
House after Arthur's death. 'I shall come to London,' she told
Dolly Ponsonby, '. . . we are trying to let the house – it is too
big for me and too full of pain and sorrow.' By this time Peter,
who in later life – perhaps because he shared the same
Christian name – became more closely identified than his
brothers with the character of 'Peter Pan', was a pupil at
Berkhamsted School. Barrie wrote to him on one occasion to
say that 'I expect twenty years from now there will be a
half-holiday given at the Berkhamsted School on the 25th of
Feb. because it is the birthday of its famous pupil.'

Sylvia died only three years after her husband, leaving her
five sons in Barrie's care; a responsibility which he exercised
until the end of his life, in 1937. Occasionally, the Davies boys
found it irksome, as they grew older, to be so closely associated
with 'Peter Pan', but several of them were destined not to
shoulder the burden for long. George was killed in action

during the First World War and Michael, ('the lad who will never be old,' as Barrie once prophetically described him), was drowned while bathing, in 1921.

'Peter Pan' has been an essential part of Christmas in the theatre for most of this century, and the royalties from the play over the years have enriched the lives of the young patients at Great Ormond Street Hospital for Sick Children. The play's namesake, Peter Llewelyn Davies, became a successful publisher before his death in 1960. Writing in 1945 of his childhood, he said that he looked back '. . . with nostalgic yearnings on Egerton House and its garden, and the three short years at Berkhamsted, (long years though to a small boy), as a sort of last paradise.'

# Plays and a Picture-Guide:

# George Bernard Shaw at Ayot St. Lawrence

When George Bernard Shaw and his wife, Charlotte, moved to the New Rectory, Ayot St. Lawrence, in November 1906, it was merely a temporary measure, while they negotiated for the purchase of a house at nearby Harmer Green. The deal fell through and so it was that, forty-four years later, in November 1950, the couple's ashes were mixed together – Charlotte had died in 1943 – and scattered in the garden of the house which G.B.S. had, by now, re-named Shaw's Corner.

After their marriage in 1898, the Shaws' search for a suitable country home had taken them to live briefly in Surrey and Cornwall, before leading them to the small Hertfordshire village which is now inextricably linked with G.B.S. Although it originally became his home more by accident than design, Shaw soon found that Ayot St. Lawrence possessed several great advantages. It was reasonably close to London, but still a sufficiently out-of-the-way spot, when he first moved there, to deter journalists and other unwanted visitors from finding him. Also, he saw in the village churchyard a tombstone over the grave of Mary Ann South, 1825–1895, bearing the inscription: 'Her time was short'. 'I thought that if it could be truthfully said of a woman who lived to be seventy years old that her time was short,' declared Shaw, 'then this was just exactly the climate for me.'

*The entrance to Shaw's Corner, Ayot St. Lawrence.*

Bernard Shaw was fifty, and already an internationally acclaimed author and playwright, when he moved to Ayot St. Lawrence. Nevertheless, it was in the hut tucked away at the bottom of the Shaw's Corner garden, that he created many of his most famous plays and characters. The hut – or 'the shelter where I write dramas helter-skelter', as Shaw described it in some deliberately bad verse – was designed to revolve, so that it always caught the sun. It was here that he wrote 'Androcles and the Lion', 'St. Joan', 'The Apple-Cart' and, perhaps what has become his most famous play of all, 'Pygmalion'. It was first performed in 1913 and spawned the immensely successful 1950s musical, 'My Fair Lady'.

Throughout their married life, the Shaws maintained a home in London, where they both spent a part of each week. Mrs Shaw enjoyed town life more than her husband, and she would sometimes stay on at their flat in Adelphi Terrace and, later, at Whitehall Court, when G.B.S. had retreated to Hertfordshire. He seemed to prefer being in the country whenever possible. 'People bother me,' he said, adding that Ayot St. Lawrence was the ideal place 'to hide away from them.'

Ayot St. Lawrence is still a delightful village today, unspoilt by the growth of nearby Welwyn Garden City. There are many fine old cottages (Shaw thought the Tudor cottage next to the Old Rectory '. . . was a lesson in village architecture'), the 'Brocket Arms' public house, originally called the 'Three Horseshoes' and over four hundred years old, and the ruins of the fourteenth-century church, with its battlemented tower. When Shaw first arrived, the village was without mains water, gas or electricity, and was not served by any public transport. 'It is a queer place,' said Shaw, 'it is a quiet sort of village, and the last thing of real importance that happened here was, perhaps, the Flood.'

*Cottages at Ayot St.Lawrence.*

At first, Shaw was regarded with a certain amount of suspicion by some of his neighbours, and he inevitably attracted a great deal of local gossip. He was known as the man 'who came from over the hill',because he didn't hunt or shoot or attend church. His religious and political opinions were always regarded as highly unorthodox, and sometimes provoked the most bizarre speculation. At the beginning of the First World War, for example, there were even fears that he might be a German spy. Apparently, these arose simply from the fact that a light could often be seen burning in a room at the top of his house, causing some people to wonder if he might be helping enemy 'planes to navigate at night! During the winter of 1915, however, following the severe blizzards which affected Hertfordshire badly at that time, Shaw joined with his neighbours to help clear the snow from blocked roads. This gained him a great deal of respect and, from that point, so far as the villagers were concerned, his star was in the ascendant. By the time of his death, he had long been held in great esteem as a much-loved member of the local community.

Shaw himself had no illusions about the effect his presence created at first in Ayot St. Lawrence. He made a speech on one occasion, to the Ayot Women's Institute in which he recalled, more in affection than in anger, that it had taken him fourteen years to be accepted in the village. 'They treated me as an interloper and suspicious stranger,' he said, 'for fourteen years.'

Shaw's Hertfordshire neighbours saw a very different side to him, in general, from that usually displayed to the outside world. To the public at large, whose only acquaintance with G.B.S. was through the newspapers and newsreels, he could often appear irascible and sometimes downright rude. To his small household staff at Shaw's Corner, however, and to the villagers of Ayot, he was almost invariably courteous and often kind-hearted. Both Shaw and his wife inspired affection and great loyalty in their employees, most of whom stayed with the couple to give many years of devoted service.

Mr and Mrs Higgs were gardener and housekeeper respectively at Shaw's Corner from 1906 until the mid-1940s, and they only retired when Mrs Higgs's health failed. In 1940, Shaw dedicated one of his books to them, touchingly inscribed: 'To Harry and Clara Higgs . . . without their friendly services I should not have had time to write my books and plays nor had any comfort in my daily life.' Perhaps it was upon Mrs Jisbella Lyth, however, a former Ayot St. Lawrence postmistress, that Shaw bestowed the greatest compliment it is in a playwright's power to give. She inspired him in the writing of his play, 'The Village Wooing', which starred Sybil Thorndike in Mrs Lyth's part, when it was produced in London in 1934.

*The Old Post Office, Ayot St. Lawrence.*

One of Shaw's great pleasures, when he was at home in Ayot St. Lawrence, was to walk in the quiet and secluded lanes around the village. More than one of his old neighbours recalled seeing him, arms resting on a field gate and lost deep in thought during his rambles. He often walked up to six miles a day, even into his late eighties. During the very severe winter of 1947, when snow lay several feet thick in Ayot St. Lawrence as elsewhere in the country, Shaw persisted in going out for his long walks. '. . . with sacks tied around his feet and halfway up his legs,' and seemingly oblivious, by all accounts, to the fact that he was ninety-one years of age.

When Shaw wanted to avoid the unwelcome attention of sightseers, who became an increasing problem for him over the years even at Ayot St. Lawrence, he would walk in the garden with Charlotte for hours on end, habitually following a favourite well-trodden route, and placing a pebble on a certain window-sill each time they passed it, to measure the distance they had covered. During his final years, when he was left on his own after his wife's death, Shaw seldom ventured outside his grounds at all, so fearful was he of being ambushed by tourists or members of the press anxious to catch a glimpse of him.

Perhaps one of Bernard Shaw's greatest interests – other than his work – was photography, and so it was entirely appropriate that his last book, completed within a few days of the fall which precipitated his death, should have been his 'Rhyming Picture Guide to Ayot St. Lawrence'. It was a slim volume (published price 1/-), containing Shaw's own photographs of local village scenes; to each of which he added a caption, written in deliberately bad verse. The preparation of it must have occupied a great deal of his time during his final summer, and it was very much a labour of love. The book was a fitting and wholly affectionate tribute to the small Hertfordshire village which had been his home for forty years.

In September 1950, Shaw fell from a small ladder while pruning some trees in his garden, and broke a leg. He was ninety-four and obviously misguided in tackling such a job at his advanced age. Although he made a good recovery at first, complications developed and, by early November, he was dead. His ashes were mixed with Charlotte's and scattered in the garden where the couple had spent so many happy hours, walking and talking together.

Shaw bequeathed his house to the National Trust, and it is now regularly open to visitors. Although more on the beaten track than in Shaw's time, the house itself has remained virtually unchanged since the playwright's death. His study still contains old notebooks, working equipment and personal mementos from the many celebrated figures – including T E Lawrence and Lady Gregory – who were his friends, and who visited him over the years at Ayot St. Lawrence.

'This is my dell and this my dwelling,' wrote Shaw, under a photograph of his house and garden, in the 'Rhyming Picture Guide':

>'Their charm so far beyond my telling,
>That though in Ireland is my birthplace,
>This home shall be my final earthplace.'

And so it was.

# Mrs Humphry Ward:

## A Friend in Need at Aldbury

Tolstoy described Mrs Humphry Ward as 'the greatest living novelist,' after her book, 'Robert Elsmere' appeared in 1888. Sales exceeding 70,000 copies in Britain alone during its first year of publication, and of almost half a million in the U.S.A., made it one of the outstanding literary successes of the nineteenth century. However, although she was a prolific writer for over forty years, Mrs Ward is largely unknown to the general reader today. Tastes change, of course, and although 'Robert Elsmere' has stood the test of time few, if any, of her other books have enjoyed the same degree of longevity. However, a minor revival of interest in her work during recent years has led to the re-issue of some of her novels – including 'Marcella' and 'Helbeck of Bannisdale' – by leading publishers.

Mrs Humphry Ward was born Mary Augusta Arnold, in 1851, at Hobart, Tasmania. She was the grand-daughter of the celebrated Dr Arnold of Rugby, and a niece of the poet, Matthew Arnold. When her family returned to England in 1856 they settled in Oxford, where Mary was brought up. It was here that she met Humphry Ward, a Fellow of Brasenose College, and they were married in 1872. They remained in Oxford until 1881, when Humphry Ward took up a post on 'The Times', and the family – by now they had three children – moved to London.

Once settled in Russell Square, (later they moved to Grosvenor Place), the Wards rented a number of country houses for their annual holidays, before taking a lease on Stocks in 1892. Situated just a short distance from the village of Aldbury, near Tring, this fine Georgian house – built in 1772 – became Mrs Ward's country home for the rest of her life. She had fallen in love with the place on her first visit. 'At Stocks I shall be able to see something of the genuine English country life,' she wrote to her brother, '. . . It has such an old walled garden, such a beautiful lime avenue, such delicious hollies and oaks, such woods behind it and about it.' Although Humphry Ward was, by now, a leader writer and, subsequently, an art critic on 'The Times', it is some indication of his wife's earning power as a novelist – during the years following the publication of 'Robert Elsmere' – that they felt able to take a lease at £400 a year, on a 'second' home in the country.

*Stocks, at Aldbury, is now a hotel and country-club.*
*(Photo: by kind permission of the proprietors.)*

Measured by any standards, Mrs Ward had always been a formidable Victorian lady, with a strong personality and robust health to match but, during her first summer at Stocks, in 1892, she fell victim to a mysterious illness which caused her a great deal of internal pain and occasionally immobilized her. Although she was to live for almost another thirty years, this complaint was never satisfactorily diagnosed, and the distressing symptoms recurred at intervals throughout the rest of her life. During the summer of 1893, she even allowed herself to be carried up and down stairs at Stocks, so severe was the pain she suffered. 'But,' she wrote to a close friend, in her usual indomitable style, 'it is not dangerous and need not prevent my working.'

In spite of her increasingly uncertain health, however, and the material and intellectual richness of her own life, Mrs Ward was not only a prolific writer, but a notable philanthropist and an active campaigner for causes she considered worthwhile. She worked quite tirelessly, for many years, on behalf of the poor in London's East End, where her single greatest achievement was probably the founding of the Passmore Edwards Settlement – later re-named Mary Ward House – which opened at Tavistock Square, Bloomsbury, in 1897. Here, under one roof, could be found accommodation, a children's play centre, a gymnasium, facilities for various clubs and classes and, on an adjacent site, a school specially designed for physically handicapped children. Such social provisions were, in the late nineteenth century, highly innovatory, and a direct result of Mrs Ward's efforts.

Stocks also played its part in the lives of these underprivileged children and adults. Mrs Ward arranged for hampers to be sent down regularly from the Stocks vegetable garden to the Settlement's kitchens, so that the meals provided there could be supplemented with fresh vegetables whenever possible. And, at Stocks itself, the two contrasting worlds that Mrs Ward inhabited sometimes drew very close to each other (although, one suspects, never quite together).

Some years after first leasing the property, the Wards bought the main house and the two cottages set in its grounds; thereby creating a small enclave of their own. One of these cottages, known at Stocks Cottage, and nestling '. . . among the steep hanging woods of Moneybury Hill,' was reserved for the use of guests and friends; (Bernard Shaw stayed there during the spring of 1896, and described it as '. . . a lonely cottage on a remote hillside'). The second cottage was set aside for the use of visitors from the East End; children or adults whom Mrs Ward felt would benefit from a day's outing, or perhaps a week's holiday or convalescence in the country under the supervision of a matron, Mrs Dell. Aldous Huxley, who was a nephew of Mrs Ward's, and a frequent visitor to the house, recalled '. . . children hopping around the shrubbery on crutches and . . how, in spite of their infirmities, they could intimidate young Wards and Huxleys by their fierce Cockney mirth!'

Although philanthropic work, and the many causes in which she took an active interest, occupied so much of her time – she was, for example, a founder member of the Women's Anti-Suffrage League – Mrs Ward considered herself to be primarily a writer. A large proportion of her novels were written at Stocks, and this was despite the many distractions that were usually on hand there. In London, she had become a noted 'Society' hostess and so, inevitably, her weekends and holidays in Hertfordshire were often crammed with visitors. Henry James, the Asquiths, the Rothschilds and many other leading public figures were among her regular guests. Nevertheless, Mrs Ward always found time to write at the beginning of the day and, after taking a drive in the country, during the late afternoon and evening as well.

In two of her novels, 'Marcella' and 'The Story of Bessie Costrell', both of which were written within a few years of moving to Stocks, Mrs Ward incorporated local incidents into the plots. For 'Marcella', she used the story of an Aldbury man who had been hanged after shooting a gamekeeper in Ashridge Park, an area of beechwoods rising above the village. She also described, in some detail, the local nineteenth-century cottage industry of straw-plaiting. In 'Bessie Costrell', she used the story of a woman who had drowned herself in the public well at Aldbury. Both of these incidents were still fresh in local memory when Mrs Ward heard about them from some of the older residents, in the course of her drives around the village.

*Sixteenth century yeoman's house and the church of St. John the Baptist, with the tall-chimneyed communal bake-house at Aldbury. (Photo: Eric Holland.)*

By the outbreak of the First World War, Mrs Ward was approaching old-age and in far from good health. Nevertheless, she made her own characteristically vigorous war effort. She drew up extensive plans for the Stocks gardens, so that sufficient fruit and vegetables would be produced to share with the village and to maintain the regular hampers to the Settlement's kitchens. A cow was put out to graze on the Stocks cricket pitch, to provide fresh milk.

Mrs Ward's literary output during the war years was no less than astonishing. She wrote eight novels between 1914 and 1918, some of which were specifically designed as 'morale boosters'. A further three books appeared over the next two years; the last of which, 'Harvest', was published after her death. By this time, however, her popularity as a writer was in decline. A contemporary critic, writing in 1910, had already described her novels as having '. . . about the same relation to first-class fiction that maps and atlases bear to great paintings.' It was a harsh judgement, perhaps, and in stark contrast to Tolstoy's assessment just over twenty years earlier.

Mrs Humphry Ward died in London during the spring of 1920, in a room which had been filled with flowers from her garden at Stocks. In 1910, she had written to a friend to say that her life was too crowded, and that she hoped '. . . there may be time left for some resting, watching years at the end of it all – when one may sit in the chimney-corner, look on, and think'. It was simply not in Mrs Ward's nature for that ever really to be the case but, over the years, Stocks had become '. . . the place of consolation which repaid her for all the fatigues and troubles of her life.'

Mrs Ward was buried in the churchyard at Aldbury, '. . . within sight of the long sweep of hill and beechwoods that she had loved so well,' after a funeral address in which Dean Inge had described her as 'perhaps the greatest Englishwoman of our time.'

*A familiar view of the village-green and stocks at Aldbury. (Photo: Eric Holland.)*

# Loose Ends (1)

## H.E. Bates

H.E. Bates was born at Rushden, Northamptonshire, in 1905, and the outlying country on and over the border into Bedfordshire is as redolent of his lovable old rogue of a character, Uncle Silas, as the hop-fields of Kent conjure up the exuberant Larkins.

Bates's family was steeped in Rushden's boot and shoe industry but 'H.E.' – as he was always known – broke with tradition. After working as a clerk and a newspaper cub reporter he found early success – at the age of twenty – as a writer, with the publication of his first novel. For almost half a century, he produced a steady stream of enormously popular novels and short stories and, tucked away in his impressive output is the earthy, country character based on his Great Uncle Joseph of Sharnbrook; a man who, born in the 1840s lived to be over ninety, and was a fixture in H.E.'s childhood.

Many a north Bedfordshire village and hamlet – Shelton, Knotting, Felmersham, Souldrop – struts its hour in the tales of Uncle Silas whose home, a thatched cottage in Barleycroft Lane, smells '. . . of old wine and tea and the earthy smell of Uncle Silas himself.'

## Christopher Fry

The playwright, Christopher Fry, enjoyed great success in the post-war British theatre, and on the international stage, not least perhaps with 'The Lady's Not for Burning', which was directed by Sir John Gielgud in the West End in 1949. The first of his plays to be published, 'The Boy With a Cart', had been written ten years earlier for a village church festival, but he had already appeared in print long before that. As a boy, he had the satisfaction of seeing one of his first attempts at writing published in the pages of 'The Bedfordshire Times'.

Christopher Fry was only six when he moved with his mother and Aunt Ada to Gladstone Street, then on the outskirts of Bedford, in 1913. The years he spent in the town, where from 1918 to 1926 he was a pupil at Bedford Modern School, were nostalgically evoked decades later, in his book, 'Can You Find Me. A Family History', which was published in 1978.

Following the advent of the 'Angry Young Men' during the mid-1950s, Christopher Fry successfully adapted to changing tastes by writing scripts for films and television. He has also gained a reputation over the years for his translations of Anouilh and Giraudoux and, in 1962, he was awarded the Queen's Gold Medal for Poetry.

# Henry Longhurst

When Henry Longhurst died, in 1978, most of the obituary notices – while acknowledging his unique style and consummate skill as a golf commentator – sought to lay emphasis on his undoubted mastery as a writer about the sport. He was the 'Sunday Times' golf correspondent for forty years; a role that he also played in the 'Evening Standard' and 'The Tatler' until the outbreak of the Second World War. His style on the printed page inevitably reflected the man: witty, interesting, serious but not solemn and, above all, demonstrating immense knowledge and enjoyment of his chosen sport.

Henry Longhurst was born at Bromham, in 1909, a village which he described candidly as 'one of the prettiest in a not very pretty county.' He retained a life-long connection with Bedford, however, through his chairmanship of the family firm, Longhurst and Skinner, but writing and commentating on golf took him all over the world.

In addition to his prolific journalism, Henry Longhurst also wrote at least a dozen books. Two of the titles, 'It was Good while it Lasted', and a volume of autobiography called 'My Life and Soft Times', provide a neat commentary in themselves on his general philosophy.

# Ewart Milne

The poet, Ewart Milne, was an Irishman who spent the last twenty years of his life at Bedford. Born in Dublin on May 25th 1903, he started writing during the 1930s, while working as a merchant seaman. After driving an ambulance in Spain during the Civil War, he returned to Dublin where his first volume of poems, 'Forty North Fifty West', was published in 1938.

Ewart Milne moved to England in 1942, spurred on by a desire to help with the war effort. He worked as a land manager at Assington Hall in Suffolk; a county in which he farmed until the early 1960s. He was a prolific poet, and volumes of his work appeared at intervals over a period of more than forty years.

To a large extent Milne ploughed his own furrow, happily acknowledging that his poetry was often outside the mainstream of contemporary fashion and – in terms of approach and subject-matter – more in the tradition of the likes of Blake and Hardy. As a result, he attracted less notice than he deserved although, by the time he died in January 1987, interest in his work was growing.

# Capt. W E Johns

Of all the many fictional schoolboy heroes who have risen to prominence during the course of this century, few can have had a greater or more lasting impact than Biggles, the ace-pilot. His creator, William Earl Johns – better known as Captain W.E. Johns – was born in 1893 at Bengeo, a suburb of Hertford. For four decades from 1932, when the first Biggles adventure appeared, Johns wrote about his most famous character in almost one hundred books. Over the years, Biggles has been serialised on the radio and television and –

more recently – he has been transferred to the cinema.

W.E. Johns also created two other long-running characters: Worrals of the WAAF (something of a female counterpart to Biggles) and Gimlet, a soldier-hero of the Commandos. In addition, he wrote adult thrillers, romances and science fiction novels, producing an overall total of one hundred and sixty-eight books during his prolific writing career, not including countless short stories and journalism. For seven years, from 1932, he was also editor of the aviation magazine, 'Popular Flying'.

W.E. Johns attended Hertford Grammar School and 'Biggles Goes to School', published in 1951, which finds our hero being educated in Norfolk, is thought to be partly autobiographical. When Johns left school, he was apprenticed to a municipal surveyor, and he later found work as a sanitary inspector at Swaffham.

With the outbreak of the First World War, Johns joined the Norfolk Yeomanry. It was only when he transferred to the Royal Flying Corps, however, that he began his long association with the service from which would emerge – judging by the number of different translations in which the Biggles books have appeared – what, at one time, was probably the most popular children's hero in the world.

# Lewis Grassic Gibbon

Lewis Grassic Gibbon's trilogy, 'A Scots Quair', has been hailed as a masterpiece of twentieth-century Scottish literature. Published between 1932–4, this saga set in north-east Scotland, from the Great War to the 'hungry thirties', is the cornerstone of Gibbon's reputation today. It was written, surprisingly enough, not in the far north but in the suburban atmosphere of Welwyn Garden City, where Gibbon spent the last years of his all-too short life.

Born James Leslie Mitchell, at Hillhead of Segget, Auchterless, in 1901, and brought up in the Mearns, south-west of Stonehaven, he had a varied career in journalism and the Services, before moving to Hertfordshire at the age of thirty. By that time his first book, 'Hanno: or the

Future of Exploration' had already appeared, together with a novel, 'Stained Radiance' and a number of short stories. His reputation was growing and he was attracting considerable attention.

It was with the writing of 'Sunset Song', the first part of 'A Scots Quair', that Mitchell adopted the pseudonym of Lewis Grassic Gibbon – derived from his mother's maiden name – thereby establishing a dual career for himself and two separate identities in the minds of his readers.

Leslie Mitchell – an erudite man: well-read and, by courtesy of the Services, widely travelled – wrote non-fiction works of historical and archaeological interest, including 'The Conquest of the Maya', published in 1934 and 'Spartacus', which had appeared a year earlier. Lewis Grassic Gibbon concentrated on works of Scottish interest and inspiration. Inevitably, the two roles occasionally overlapped and never more so than in 'Nine against the Unknown', a collection of biographies of famous explorers published in 1934 and co-written by Mitchell and Gibbon!

During the few years he lived at Welwyn Garden City, first at Edgars Court and later at 107 Handside Lane, Mitchell's work-load was truly breathtaking, and thirteen of his books – many of them requiring detailed research – appeared between 1932–4. Nevertheless, he still found time to enjoy a happy family life with his wife and children, and to form the Twelve Club: a debating group which met locally every week, and whose members included an M.P., a number of journalists, a musician and other kindred spirits.

Mitchell was as hard at work as ever, and full of plans for future books when, in February 1935, he died of peritonitis after an emergency operation. A writer of proven achievement and immense promise, he found a unique voice during his short career and, in 'A Scots Quair', produced a major work of lasting significance.

# By Hot-Air and Horseback:

## Colonel Fred Burnaby of Bedford

In some respects, the life story of Colonel Fred Burnaby might have been lifted straight out of the pages of the 'Boys' Own Paper'. An Army Officer, hot-air balloonist, parliamentary candidate, journalist and travel-writer; he was a flamboyant, almost literally larger-than-life figure, whose brave exploits and military derring-do seemed to mark him out, from the very beginning, for a hero's death at an early age. It was a destiny he fulfilled in January 1885, when he was 'smitten in the throat' during a battle in the Sudan. He was forty-three.

Yet below the surface, however, there lurked a contradiction in the apparently robust and vigorous man, who was plagued by debilitating intestinal trouble for much of his life. The man who was reputed to be the strongest in the British Army – some said in the whole of Europe – and about whom apocryphal stories regarding his prowess were legion – was frequently laid low by complaints of the liver and, later, by weakness of the lungs and heart.

Frederick Gustavus Burnaby – the name itself commands

attention – was born in March 1842. His father was rector of St. Peter's Church, Bedford, and owned property in Leicestershire. He was an autocratic, but a fair-minded man; a fox-hunting parson, it was said, 'of the old school.' Young Fred, one suspects, would have caused something of a stir at the rectory. He was a boisterous lad, who enjoyed nothing better than diving into a nearby pond and '. . . coming out green all over,' or practising with dumb-bells to develop his muscles, in the rectory drawing-room.

*St. Peter's church, Bedford.*

Fred Burnaby was sent to Bedford Grammar School at the age of nine, but a year later found him at a private school near Stamford and, shortly afterwards, at Harrow. Within two years, however, he had gone north to Oswestry, studying under the brother of the vicar of St. Paul's, Bedford. From Shropshire he went to Dresden to study languages, and he returned to England at the age of sixteen, fluent in German, French and Italian. The peripatetic nature of his education set the tone for the rest of his life. In September 1859, having long since decided that he would not follow his father into the Church, he joined the Royal Horse Guards, and embarked upon a distinguished army career.

Fred Burnaby began writing in the late 1860s when, together with two literary-minded friends, he established a 'Society' newspaper. It was called 'Vanity Fair'; a title thought up by Fred and no doubt inspired by his close acquaintance – which was inevitable given his Bedford childhood – with Bunyan's 'Pilgrim's Progress'.

Burnaby's earliest sustained literary efforts, therefore, were a series of letters published in 'Vanity Fair', and written from Spain in 1868–9. They appeared under the general title, 'Out of Bounds', and were signed 'Convalescent'. Burnaby who, by this time, had risen to the rank of Captain, had travelled to Spain in order to recuperate from a spell of ill-health. But as a country on the edge of revolution, however, it also appealed to the military man in him. 'In Spain,' he declared, 'there will be no lack of excitement and I shall have every opportunity of studying my profession.' His letters were intended to give the reader at home a general picture of Spanish life and customs, 'more than you will see,' explained Burnaby, perhaps not over modestly, 'in any books published on Spain . . .'

Later, Burnaby engaged in more serious journalistic work. In 1874 he went as the military correspondent of 'The Times', again to Spain, where he reported on the Carlist War, and formed a lasting friendship with Don Carlos himself, in the process. Towards the end of that year, once more at the request of 'The Times', he made his first visit to the Sudan, the scene of his eventual demise. Here, he joined up with his military hero, Gordon, and journeyed far up the Nile with him.

During the course of this assignment, Burnaby learnt in Khartoum that the Russian Government was refusing Europeans entry into Central Asia; a situation which led to his book, 'A Ride to Khiva'. It was to be the first of several books, in fact, from which Burnaby's reputation as a travel writer of sorts grew.

Being of a 'contradictorious spirit', the embargo on Europeans was intolerable to Burnaby, and he determined to defy the ruling by travelling to the town of Khiva. He was not acting merely out of sheer cussedness; he genuinely wanted to discover what lay behind the prohibition. Back in London, Burnaby consulted with various officials and, having been granted leave from the army, he set off – in late November 1875

– into the intense cold of a severe Russian winter. Arriving at St. Petersburg, he was told, 'Get to Khiva? You might as well try to get to the moon.' But, astronaut that he was, Burnaby achieved his objective after crossing the Khivan desert in sub-zero temperatures.

'A Ride to Khiva' was a detailed account of this 3,000 mile journey made largely on horseback, and it became a best-seller when it appeared in 1876. Dated though it now inevitably seems, both in style and attitudes, the book was given a new lease of life in 1983, when Century Publishing reprinted it, with an Introduction by Eric Newby.

In 1877, Burnaby repeated his success with a second book, evocatively entitled 'On Horseback in Asia Minor'. At this remove, the reason for his five-months' journey – undertaken during a long spell of winter leave and begun in November 1876 – is of less interest, perhaps, than the fact that he actually accomplished it. It was a journey of '. . . over 13,000 miles,' he told his mother in a letter, during February 1877, 'and all on horseback . . ' 'I have got very thin,' he reported to his sister, later that same month, adding that Radford, his devoted servant, a trooper in the Royal Horse Guards, was reduced to 'a walking skeleton'. Safely back in England during the spring, however, he immediately set about writing an account of his adventures, and the result was 'On Horseback in Asia Minor'.

One of Burnaby's enduring passions was hot-air ballooning, an activity which, on more than one occasion, threatened to anticipate what would, in any event, be a premature death. His enthusiasm had been fired initially by a visit to Cremorne Gardens in Chelsea, where he was just in time to witness final preparations for an ascent of the largest hot-air balloon ever constructed. Somehow, in his inimitable fashion, he managed to hitch a lift, and helped with the stoking during the voyage over London.

Two years later, Burnaby made an ascent from Windsor, with an army friend who had his own balloon. Within a few hours, they were gliding at two thousand feet over Bedford, where Fred's father happened to be at work in his garden. 'I should not be surprised if my boy were in that car,' old Mr Burnaby remarked to a companion, who was standing nearby.

Later that evening Fred arrived at the rectory, having landed safely eight miles from Bedford!

It was inevitable that, one day, Burnaby would attempt a channel crossing by hot-air balloon, in the hope of succeeding where others before had failed. It was a feat he accomplished in a solo trip lasting four-and-a-quarter hours, on 23rd March 1882. The journey, which attracted a great deal of attention, was not without incident, and provided the subject for another book, 'A Ride Across the Channel and Other Adventures in the Air', which was published later that same year.

Two years earlier, despite increasing ill-health, Fred Burnaby had stood – unsuccessfully – as a Conservative candidate at Birmingham, in the Parliamentary elections of 1880. Whether or not he might have eventually become a politician – after leaving the army – it is impossible to judge; and his poor state of health must have cast some doubt on such a prospect. Fate, however, had other more definite plans in store for him.

In January 1885, Fred – now Colonel – Burnaby, was killed while on active service in the Sudan. Sensing that he might not survive this particular expedition, to effect the long-delayed rescue of General Gordon, he had re-visited old haunts at Bedford before leaving England. He looked up old friends and hinted that he might not see them again. He wandered around the rectory garden, '. . . where the old house and St. Peter's Church peeped at him through their foliage, just as they had done in his boyhood.'

Burnaby left behind him an unfinished political novel, 'Our Radicals', which appeared posthumously in 1886. Perhaps the military correspondent and travel writer believed that he might turn novelist, although it seems unlikely. Essentially, Burnaby was a warrior and a man of action, whose writing grew out of a soldier's life.

# Flints and Fungi:

## Worthington George Smith at Dunstable

It was entirely in character with Worthington George Smith that the chill which – later developing into pneumonia – led to his death, should have been contracted while he was out researching an article in Dunstable – at the age of eighty-two! Indefatigable until the last, he could truly be said to have died with a pen in his hand, in keeping with the epitaph he had composed for himself: 'His labours are now at an end . . . and if ever a man deserved to rest in peace it is Worthington George Smith.'

W.G.S. – for, like George Bernard Shaw, he became instantly recognisable by his initials, and he shared with G.B.S. both a life-long abstinence from strong drink and the capacity to walk long distances in old-age – was already fifty by the time that he moved into The Hawthorns, at 121 High Street South, Dunstable. Sadly, the house is no longer to be seen; it was demolished in 1959, during a building re-development programme.

Although Worthington Smith was born at Aske Street,

Shoreditch, in 1835, and had lived all his life in London, his family's roots were elsewhere. His father, George Smith, a Civil Servant working in the capital, came from the Hertfordshire village of Gaddesden Row, almost on the border with Bedfordshire, and there were family connections with several other villages in the area. Smith's mother, Sarah Worthington, came from Laxton, in Nottinghamshire.

When Worthington Smith left school, he trained initially to be an architect, and was apprenticed first to a Mr Johnson, off the Strand and, later, to Sir Horace Jones. He spent several years designing ecclesiastical furniture and prepared drawings for some illustrious projects, including the restoration of Westminster Abbey. Despite the importance of some of this work, however, (and, given that Smith won prizes for several of his designs, his obvious ability, too), he found the job curiously unsatisfying.

In 1858, Worthington Smith decided to abandon architecture altogether, and to make his living as an illustrator. It was a brave decision for a young married man of twenty-three, with the imminent prospect of a growing family to support. Initially making good use of his architectural training, he supplied illustrations to a periodical called 'The Builder'. Before long, however, harnessing the interest in fungi and plant forms which he had developed as a diversion from the drawing-board, he was contributing botanical illustrations to a variety of gardening and horticultural publications.

Worthington Smith's reputation grew rapidly. In 1865, he was awarded the Royal Horticultural Society's Banksian Gold Medal and, later, he became Chief Illustrator of 'The Gardener's Chronicle' and editor of 'The Floral Magazine'. In 1867, a year before he was elected a Fellow of the Linnean Society, Smith's first book, 'Mushrooms and Toadstools: How to distinguish poisonous fungi', appeared. Although he received very little money for the work, it sold well and quickly went into a second edition, thereby enhancing Smith's reputation as an authority on the subject.

Other botanical works followed throughout Worthington Smith's life and occasionally, it must be said, almost to its cost. Smith was a confirmed advocate of what might be termed 'hands-on' research and, even as an elderly man of seventy-five, when preparing his 'Edible and Poisonous Fungi' guide for the Natural History Museum, in 1910, he tested the various samples of fungi simply by eating them! Although this method occasioned a few ill-effects, that he actually survived it is a tribute to his profound knowledge of the subject.

When Worthington Smith moved to Dunstable, it was not quite the random choice which it might at first appear. As a child, he had become familiar with many nearby villages, when visiting his father's relatives, and his wife, Henrietta, had been born in the town. When Smith developed a heart condition towards the end of 1884, and his doctor strongly advised a move away from London, Dunstable seemed the obvious choice.

*Worthington Smith's home (demolished in 1959) at 121 High Street South, Dunstable. (Photo: by kind permission of the White Crescent Press Ltd.)*

The small, south Bedfordshire town had much to recommend it, however, beyond mere family associations. During the 1870s, Smith's inveterately curious mind had turned its attention to archaeology when, in 1878, he had discovered some splinters of Palaeolithic flint on a building-site in Stoke Newington. This fired him to conduct further research elsewhere and when, seven years later, he found similar fragments embedded in some gravel at Dunstable, whilst house-hunting there with Henrietta, he must have thought – correctly as it turned out – that it augured well for his future in the town.

Worthington Smith had several important projects in hand when he moved to The Hawthorns. There was Dr Stevens's two-volume work, 'British Fungi', to be illustrated, and material to be prepared for a new edition of Encyclopaedia Britannica, on both fungi and Bedfordshire! Smith's own book, 'Diseases of Field and Garden Crops' had recently appeared, and he was still contributing regularly – as he would do until 1910 – to 'The Gardener's Chronicle'.

Whenever time allowed, however, Worthington Smith would strike out in the general direction of Gaddesden Row, Caddington, or some other village to the south-east of Dunstable, in the hope of making further important archaeological discoveries. His most exciting find was probably made in March 1890, as he described four years later in his influential book, 'Man the Primeval Savage', when he discovered a Palaeolithic working and living place – a site where flint tools were actually manufactured – at Caddington. Despite the undoubted significance of this discovery, however, seldom could a week have passed by without Smith carrying something home.

Thomas Bagshawe, writing in 'Bedfordshire Magazine' in 1967, recalled his childhood visits to The Hawthorns. 'The inside of the house was like an Aladdin's Cave to a youthful archaeologist,' he wrote. 'Except for the parlour at the back, the house was chock-full with antiquarian objects, including skeletons and cremation burials. This was apart from books, periodicals, finished and unfinished drawings . . '

Worthington Smith's knack of making important discoveries – whether skeletons from burial-mounds or old Stone Age flints – was by no means confined to the field of archaeology. Asked in 1899 to do some research for the local council, he was combing the British Museum Manuscript Department and the Public Records Office for ancient charters. During his investigations, he unearthed what is arguably the most important document in Dunstable's history: the Charter granted 'to the Church of the Blessed Peter at Dunestapel', by William the Conqueror's son, Henry I.

During his late sixties, Worthington Smith received two marks of public recognition which gave him particular pleasure. In 1902, he was awarded a Civil List Pension of £50 a year, 'in consideration of his services to archaeology and botanical illustration.' Granted by the Monarch on the advice of the Prime Minister, the Pension was a welcome addition to the purse of a man whose income – although adequate – by no means reflected his distinction.

Then, in 1903, Smith was made First Freeman of the Borough of Dunstable, in appreciation of his services to the town. 'Of all the honours, this has been the least expected,' he said, in his speech of thanks, 'and now that it is given, I can truly say that it is the most welcome testimony of respect that could possibly have been bestowed upon me.'

Before long, Worthington Smith was more than able to reciprocate the gesture when, in 1904, he published his comprehensive guide-book, 'Dunstable: Its History and Surroundings'. Subsequently unavailable for many years, it was reprinted by Bedfordshire County Council in 1980. Much had changed in the town, of course, during the years which had elapsed since the book first appeared, but with its original photographs and section of contemporary advertisements, it remains not only an invaluable record of Dunstable at the beginning of the century, but also an important history of the town.

Worthington Smith carried on working until the end of his life. In 1907, the Trustees of the British Museum published his most specialized – and entirely scientific – work, a 'Synopsis of British Basidiomycetes'. It was another survey of fungi, which had taken him seventeen years to prepare for publication. His active interest in archaeology also continued undiminished and – well into his seventies – he made several further important discoveries of Palaeolithic land sites in the Dunstable area.

Those who knew him personally attest to Worthington Smith's kindliness and marked lack of pretension; a man who would never pass a tramp or field labourer without a friendly word. 'I have always fraternized with the men in the fields, roads and pits,' he wrote. 'We are close friends, and always speak to each other on terms of equality. They help me, and I don't forget to help them'

When Worthington Smith died, in October 1917, he was accorded Dunstable's equivalent of a State Funeral; his remains were attended to the cemetery in West Street by the Mayor and Corporation of the town. There, he was laid to rest beside Henrietta, who had died only four months earlier after sixty-one years of marriage. W.G.S. was buried in that same earth whose '. . . secrets he treasured,' explained the Rev. Gascoyne, at the funeral service, 'not because he wished to retain them as secrets, but that he might pass them on to his fellow men, so that they might be made wise by his wisdom.' As for Worthington Smith himself, 'I like to consider all the folk of Dunstable and its neighbourhood as my friends,' he had written in his guide-book of 1904. 'All are friends round Dunstable.'

*The cemetery in West Street, Dunstable.*

# Mark Rutherford:

## A Bedford Childhood

Returning to his home at Hastings after a visit to the north of England, in the summer of 1893, William Hale White – whose pen-name was Mark Rutherford – broke his long journey at Bedford, the Cowfold and Eastthorpe of his novels. It was the town where, sixty-two years earlier, he had been born in a room above his father's printing and bookselling business in the High Street and where, by all accounts, – not least his own – he spent an extremely happy childhood.

He passed a few days revisiting old haunts with his daughter, Molly, and remembering old times; and although elderly himself, he found over at Oakley – where the family of his nurse, Jane, had lived – people yet more stricken in years, who still remembered him as a child. This sentimental journey made a great impression on him and, despite his long absence – or perhaps because of it – he felt very much as if he had come home.

There was, in fact, no practical reason why he should not return to live in Bedford if he so wished; except that going back there permanently might pierce the gossamer curtain of illusion, or perhaps the town held simply too many memories. Also, he had moved away over forty years earlier and, despite the deep emotions which this glimpse of his childhood had stirred up, his life had inevitably developed elsewhere. Yet, in one sense, it could be said that he never really left Bedford at all; a notion to which his handful of novels bears ample testimony.

Hale – as he was called by his family, to distinguish him from his father, William White – spent his early Victorian childhood in a Bedford which is much altered, of course, but still not wholly unrecognizable today, with the dominating presence of the Great Ouse making its stately serpentine – then as now – on either side and through the very heart of the town. But, looking back on it with all the perspective that old-age brings, he was conscious of his good fortune in knowing the place before it had properly exploded into the nineteenth century. 'In my boyhood,' he wrote, 'it differed, excepting an addition northwards a few years before, much less from Speed's map of 1609 than the Bedford of 1910 differs from the Bedford of 1831.' With a population of around ten thousand, the town – in Hale's young day – was only about one-eighth of its present size.

There could hardly have been a better place, he claimed, for outdoor amusements, and the lad who loved to bury his nose in a book, and to read 'Chamber's Journal' in front of the kitchen fire, also spent a great deal of his time by or on the Ouse, where there was fishing, swimming and boating (in his own little boat) to be had in abundance and, during the winter months, skating when '. . . the meadows for miles were a great lake, and there was no need to take off skates in order to get past mills and weirs.' There were potatoes, 'sweet as peaches', to be roasted in the open-air on dank November afternoons, followed by bat-fowling after dark.

It seems there was seldom a dull moment. When Hale's nurse, Jane, went home to Oakley for a holiday, she often took her 'dear boy' to stay with her family there. He loved her parents' tiny thatched cottage where everybody lived, cooked, slept and had their being in one cramped room. 'No entertainment, no special food was provided,' he recalled later, '. . . there was just the escape to a freer life.'

*The Great Ouse at Bedford – Mark Rutherford's childhood playground.*

*The bridge at Oakley.*

Hale grew to know many of the country people and the outlying villages around Bedford through his father and his uncle, Samuel Lovell. Uncle Samuel, a benevolent man, was a maltster and coal-merchant who, every once in a while, grasped the nettle and set off on a debt-collecting expedition. Many of his creditors lived on remote farms and in isolated hamlets, and his young nephew often went with him.

The counterpart to these weekday excursions occurred on Sundays, when Hale would sometimes accompany his father, who was a deacon at the Old Meeting (later called Bunyan Meeting) in Bedford, when he 'supplied' the pulpit in outlying districts. Some of the characters he met in the course of these outings survived in Hale's memory, to re-emerge on the pages of his novels many years later.

Sundays, however, were also responsible for the only dark cloud in Hale's otherwise sunny existence. When Mr White was not 'supplying' the pulpit elsewhere, the whole family attended the Old Meeting morning and evening. 'The evenings were particularly trying,' Hale recalled in old age. 'The windows of the meeting-house streamed inside with condensed breath and the air we took into our lungs was poisonous . . . do what I could it was impossible to keep awake.'

The carefree days of boating and fishing, bathing and skating, holidays at Oakley and expeditions with Uncle Lovell, all came to an end, however, when Hale was fifteen. He left school and, being destined for the Independent ministry, was sent – in 1848 – to the Countess of Huntingdon's College at Cheshunt where, he declared, 'I learnt nothing . . . and did not make a single friend.' Three years later, he was transferred to New College, St. John's Wood, from where he was swiftly expelled for expressing unorthodox and – so far as the college authorities were concerned – unacceptable views regarding the inspiration of the Bible.

The ramifications of this episode were considerable. In supporting his son over the issue, Mr White succeeded not only in alienating himself from members of the Old Meeting, but also in losing many of his book-buying customers as well; a significant number of whom were drawn from the clergy. Ultimately, his business failed and – having no better success with a tannery started in partnership with Samuel Lovell – he left Bedford for London, where his acquaintance with Lord Charles Russell had secured for him the post of Assistant Doorkeeper (and, shortly afterwards, that of Principal Doorkeeper), at the House of Commons.

Hale, in the meantime, after the briefest of encounters with the teaching profession, had settled down to work as an assistant on John Chapman's 'Westminster Review', in the Strand. It was there that he met Marian Evans (the novelist George Eliot), Chapman's assistant editor, whose intelligence and kindness made a lasting impression upon him. But the job itself did not suit him and, with the help of Samuel Whitbread, Member for Bedford, he obtained a junior clerkship in the Registrar-General's Office, at Somerset House.

Like Anthony Trollope, much of Mark Rutherford's literary work was accomplished in spite of an increasingly demanding career in the Civil Service. After a year or two he transferred to the Admiralty, where he rose to be Assistant Director of Navy Contracts, and retired after more than thirty years' service; years which had seen the publication of four of his novels, starting with 'The Autobiography of Mark Rutherford', in 1881. It was a book which he confessed later had been written under 'extraordinary high-pressure', and caused him to rise at 4.30 every morning in order to complete it!

Hale had married shortly after joining the Civil Service, and he moved out of London – where he had been lodging – to Carshalton. He was to spend the rest of his days in Surrey, Kent or Sussex, until his death at Groombridge in 1913, at the age of eighty-one. With the added expense of a young and growing family to support, he began writing mainly to supplement his secure but inadequate income. His own interest in literature, coupled with his access to Parliamentary news through his father's privileged position at the Commons, made him a sought after contributor to a variety of regional newspapers and to some national periodicals as well. His 'thinly-disguised', semi-autobiographical first novel, however, with its portrayal of the spiritual development of a young Dissenter, and its sequel, 'Mark Rutherford's Deliverance', which appeared in 1885, were well-received and gained him a loyal following.

Beyond a brief fragment of genuine autobiography, it is to

the novels themselves that one must turn for a glimpse of Bedford in Mark Rutherford's childhood; a town which he described as 'the country a little thickened', and where gardens reached down to the river and fields and the limitless fens. Like Hardy's Casterbridge – or Dorchester – of the same period, 'it was the complement of the rural life around; not its urban opposite,' and a place, he said, where all the shopkeepers knew the points of a horse.

More than thirty years away from the town – busy years spent working in a London office, caring for an invalid wife and bringing up a family – had done nothing to dim the memory of those early days. If anything, his absence had served to throw them into relief, so that when 'Miriam's Schooling', 'The Revolution in Tanner's Lane', 'Clara Hopgood' and 'Catharine Furze' followed 'The Autobiography' and 'Deliverance' they each had, to some extent, a Bedfordshire setting, and were enriched by Mark Rutherford's fond memories of the place and its people.

It is in 'Catharine Furze', perhaps, that the most vivid picture of early Victorian Bedford emerges. It was a town where most of the shops still had bow-windows; where the upper-storeys of houses overhung the street and where, between eight and nine in the evening, the shop-keepers 'looked in at each other for a chat.' For Mark Rutherford it was a time in his own life, he said, '. . . when joys were enjoyed without reflection, when the forecasting of the morrow was a pure unconscious pleasure.'

# A Novel Civil Servant:

# Anthony Trollope at Waltham Cross

Anthony Trollope was one of the most popular, and certainly one of the most prolific of writers, during the second half of the nineteenth century. Although today, perhaps, his fame rests heavily on the Palliser saga and his tales of life in Barsetshire, he actually published around seventy books; the overwhelming majority of which were novels, but there were also short stories, biographies, sketches and volumes of travel writing drawn from his personal experience. It was an impressive output by any standards, and a remarkable achievement bearing in mind that Trollope spent much of his working-life as a busy – and eventually quite senior – Civil Servant, in the General Post Office. His writing, therefore, was squeezed into the relatively few hours he could devote to it early in the morning, before setting out on his official duties.

Anthony Trollope moved to Waltham Cross in the autumn of 1859. Waltham House – which he initially leased and later bought outright – was 'a rickety old place,' he said, 'requiring much repair and occasionally not as weather-tight as it should be.' A photograph taken of it at the beginning of the present century, however, shows that it was a fine-looking Georgian house set well back from the road. It was situated close to the Eleanor Cross itself but was demolished in 1930, to make way for the houses and shops needed to accommodate and serve a fast-growing population.

*Waltham House in 1910. (Photo: by kind permission of Cheshunt Library.)*

In 'An Autobiography', published after his death, Trollope described his Hertfordshire home as 'the scene of much happiness.' He was to spend twelve contented years there; years during which his writing career flourished as never before. It was also a period when, for the first time in his adult life, he was able to settle and put down roots. He had travelled widely on Post Office business over the years; to Egypt, the West Indies, the United States and, most recently, to Ireland, where he had met Rose Heseltine whom he married in 1844. It was a posting based in London, but requiring him to travel throughout the eastern counties, which eventually brought him to Waltham Cross.

Born in 1815, Anthony Trollope was forty-four when he moved to Waltham House, and hard at work on one of his

Barsetshire novels, 'Framley Parsonage', which began serialization in the 'Cornhill Magazine' in January 1860. It was a time when his pen seemed to be flowing more freely than ever, although it invariably cracked on at a fair pace. He is said, in fact, to have written more words than any other English novelist.

Trollope was also about to embark on one of the most consistently prosperous periods in his life, with his popularity as a novelist undoubtedly reaching its peak during the 1860s. These were the years which saw the publication of 'The Small House at Allington' (1864), – a Barsetshire novel which owed more than a little to its author's Hertfordshire surroundings – 'Can You Forgive Her' (1864), the first of the Palliser sequence, and 'The Last Chronicle of Barset' (1867), which Trollope himself reckoned to be among the finest of his books. Other principal novels during the palmy years at Waltham House included 'Orley Farm' (1862), 'The Claverings' (1867) and 'The Vicar of Bullhampton' (1870). He wrote, in addition countless articles – politics and hunting a speciality – for numerous periodicals.

*Grove Cottage, Cheshunt, now the site of Bishop's Court, was thought to be the original 'Small House at Allington'. (Photo: by kind permission of Cheshunt Library.)*

Anthony Trollope adopted fairly desperate measures to accommodate his mammoth literary work-load, but his method seemed to suit him well enough. He described it in 'An Autobiography'. Up by 5 o'clock every morning, he invariably began work half-an-hour later by reading through the material he had prepared the previous day. At 6am he began writing in earnest, and carried on until 9.30am. He disciplined himself to write 250 words every quarter-of-an-hour, and kept a watch in front of him on his desk in order to monitor his progress. On a normal day he would produce a quota of 2,500 words; a sufficient amount, in fact, to achieve his target of three three-volume novels a year. No doubt there were slight variations to this regime, but the basic pattern remained constant, as he had conditioned himself to produce the same number of words daily whether at home or travelling by boat or train.

There is a school of thought which suggests that Trollope's popularity declined after the publication of 'An Autobiography' simply because his readers found this approach to his craft rather too cold and mechanical. Perhaps he would have gone out of fashion anyway, for a while, after his death, but it is also possible that he contributed to his falling sales by shattering too many illusions.

Living at Waltham Cross gave Anthony Trollope a much desired opportunity to enter more fully into London's literary and social life. Before long, he was a member of the Garrick Club and The Athenaeum. At last he was able to indulge his passion for card games with like-minded companions, and he relished the opportunity for new friendships which these institutions offered. Dr Johnson would have considered him a 'clubbable' man and Trollope, whose work had sometimes caused him to lead a rather more solitary life in the past than suited him, was pleased – and surprised – to find that he was extremely popular in these circles.

Waltham Cross was also ideally placed for another of Anthony Trollope's passions: hunting. He had feared that, when he left Ireland, his hunting days would be over, but that proved to be far from the case. During his years at Waltham House he usually managed to hunt twice a week, and could even afford to keep a few suitable horses himself. By his own admission, his passion for the sport was somewhat greater than his flair; his heavy build and poor eyesight not being great assets in the field. Living in Waltham Cross but on the border with Essex and Middlesex, however, meant that he was able to hunt in three counties close to home, and '. . . few men,' he said, a touch over-modestly, perhaps, 'have investigated more closely than I have done the depth, and breadth, and water-holding capacities of an Essex ditch.'

One demanding career is usually sufficient for most people, and Trollope had two. Indeed, between his writing and the Post Office, it is difficult to visualize how he found the time – or the energy – for anything else. By 1867, however, he felt sufficiently confident of making enough money from his writing alone, to resign from the Post Office – only eight years short of qualifying for a Civil Service Pension.

Now, for the first time, Trollope was writing without the lifeline of a regular salary to underpin his literary earnings, but the income from his novels alone would have supported him in sufficient style as the 1860s wore on. No longer debarred by his Civil Servant status, however, Trollope stood – unsuccessfully – for Parliament as a Liberal, on two occasions; his interest in politics having originally spawned the Palliser novels. He also edited the 'St. Paul's Magazine' – at £1,000 a year – from 1867–70 and, with a wide circle of literary friends in London, including George Eliot and G H Lewes, he was constantly exploring new ways of bolstering his income.

Nevertheless, as the 1860s drew to a close and, despite the fact that his popularity had never been greater, Trollope instinctively felt that, sooner or later, the tide would turn, with the inevitable falling away of his income. 'The writing of novels,' he declared, 'could not go on for ever.' (As it turned out, he was to continue writing with great success for another decade.) However, with a degree of caution that was natural to him, and with an eye to economy, the decision was made – albeit reluctantly – to part with Waltham House. Matters were brought to a head when Trollope and his wife arranged to visit their son, who was sheep-farming in Australia. They would be away for at least eighteen months, and so it seemed the ideal time to sell up, and find somewhere less expensive to maintain when they returned home.

It was a considerable wrench for Trollope to leave Waltham House, the place which had enabled him to realize his ambition of living as a country gentleman. There was room to keep a few pigs and cows, and he had cultivated strawberries and peaches in the garden where, on balmy summer nights, he would sip after-dinner drinks with his guests. But, the decision made, Trollope put his house up for lease or sale, and set off with his wife to the other side of the world, leaving behind several novels to appear in his absence and having secured a contract with his publisher to write a book about his trip, while he was away.

In the event, Trollope experienced considerable difficulty in selling Waltham House, and two years passed before it was eventually bought by Mr Paul, a famous local rose-grower. Trollope claimed to have lost around £800 on the deal. 'I presume,' he wrote, 'that I am not well adapted for transactions of that kind.'

Trollope lived in central London for some years, after he returned to England in 1872, and still managed to hunt occasionally in Hertfordshire and Essex. He spent the last eighteen months of his life at South Harting, in West Sussex, and died in 1882 aged sixty-seven.

# Charles Dickens:

# The Inimitable Boz in Hertfordshire

Charles Dickens was not really a Hertfordshire man at all. That is to say, he was not born in the county and neither did he ever live there. Although he entered the world at Portsmouth, in February 1812, he belonged more properly to London, or more particularly to Gad's Hill Place, his beloved home near the Medway town of Rochester. But even in the days before railways had supplanted stage-coaches – a transformation that Dickens witnessed in his own lifetime – Hertfordshire was still only a short ride from the capital; so that England's most popular nineteenth-century writer, (for surely he was that, in the true sense of the word), knew the county well, and immortalized pockets of it in at least a handful of his novels and short stories.

Charles Dickens's earliest visit to Hertfordshire – or, at least, the first to have any significance for his later work and his biographer – was made in 1835, as a young reporter working on the influential London newspaper, 'The Morning Chronicle'. Still aged only twenty-three, his life had already been a model essay in the Samuel Smiles philosophy of self-improvement. As the son of a clerk in the Navy Payroll Office, he had not expected to begin his working life by labelling bottles in a blacking-factory at Hungerford Stairs. But his father's chronic improvidence, and inevitable bankruptcy, meant that young Dickens was forced to leave school prematurely, and take what job he could find.

By the age of fifteen, however, Dickens had started work as an office-boy with a firm of solicitors. He also began to teach himself shorthand and, by his seventeenth birthday, had become a freelance parliamentary reporter, taking down speeches in the House of Commons from a seat in the Gallery. Before long, his reputation for having the fastest and most accurate shorthand of any reporter in London – and possibly in the country – led to his position with 'The Morning Chronicle'.

In 1835, when a part of Hatfield House was destroyed by fire – an incident which claimed the life of the first Marchioness of Salisbury – Dickens was sent into Hertfordshire to report on the tragedy. The ambitious young journalist was already supplementing his income by writing descriptive sketches – these were later collected and comprised his first book, 'Sketches by Boz' – and events of this kind were all grist to his mill.

*Hatfield House, family home of the Cecils since the early seventeenth century.*

*The Eight Bells, Hatfield.*

The impression made on Dickens by that night's work found an echo, perhaps, a few years later in 'Oliver Twist', when Bill Sikes – in order to divert his mind – helped to extinguish a fire in a huddle of buildings somewhere on the road between Hatfield and St. Albans. Having murdered his girlfriend, Nancy, in Spitalfields, Sikes had 'shaped his course for Hatfield,' in a futile attempt to escape the rigours of the law. While resting at an inn, thought to be 'The Eight Bells' at the lower end of Fore Street, he had been troubled by a pedlar of the 'infallible and invaluable composition for removing . . wine-stains, fruit-stains, beer-stains, water-stains, paint-stains, pitch-stains, mud-stains . . . blood-stains!' The man offered to demonstrate his wares with the aid of Bill Sikes's blood-stained hat! It was soon after leaving the inn that Sikes encountered the fire.

Dickens had already employed his local knowledge of Hertfordshire in an earlier episode of 'Oliver Twist'. Oliver had left the workhouse where he was born – possibly at Peterborough – and was making his way southwards on foot, to London. After seven days on the road, he arrived at Barnet in the early morning. 'The window-shutters were closed; the street was empty; not a soul had awakened to the business of the day. The sun was rising in all its splendid beauty; but the light only served to show the boy his own lonesomeness and desolation, as he sat, with bleeding feet and covered with dust, upon a door-step.' Before long, Oliver was accosted and treated to a light breakfast in the tap-room of a local public-house, by Jack Dawkins, better-known to his friends as 'The Artful Dodger'. If it had not been for this encounter in Barnet, the world might well have remained in ignorance of young Oliver's existence!

Dickens returned to Hatfield in the two Christmas stories he wrote – published in 1863 and 1864 – featuring the much-loved Mrs Lirriper. Mrs Lirriper, of course, had spent her honeymoon 'and passed as happy a fortnight as ever was . . .' at 'The Salisbury Arms', a once-famous coaching-inn, at the top of Fore Street. Later, when Mr Lirriper passed away, he was buried in Hatfield churchyard. 'I . . put a sandwich and a drop of sherry in a little basket,' his widow tells us, 'and went down to Hatfield churchyard outside the coach and kissed my hand and laid it with a kind of proud and swelling love on my husband's grave . . .'

Hertfordshire has its place, too, in 'Bleak House', which was originally serialized in monthly parts from 1852–3. There are a number of specific references to the county in the text:

'Jarndyce of Bleak House, my lord,' said Mr Kenge.
'And Bleak House,' said his lordship, 'is in –'
'Hertfordshire, my lord.'

Later, when Richard Carstone, Ada Clare and Esther Summerson are making their way from London to Mr Jarndyce's house, we read that there were horses waiting for them at Barnet, but that the roads were heavy-going and delayed their progress. Thus, '. . . the long night had closed in, before we came to St. Albans; near to which town Bleak House was, we knew.'

Although Dickens has accurately established the geography of the county in 'Bleak House', much debate has surrounded the location of the actual house he had in mind when writing the novel. Several houses in St. Albans have been put forward as likely candidates over the years, including a handsome Georgian property in Catherine Street. (Dickens is reputed to have written parts of the book while staying in the town at the

'Queen's Hotel'.) However, as the prototype of Mr Jarndyce's house has also been placed at Broadstairs or Kensworth, the issue is awash with speculation.

Nevertheless, 'Bleak House' does have at least one irrefutable link with the county. When the novel appeared in volume form, in 1853, it was dedicated, by Dickens, '. . . as a remembrance of our friendly union, to my companions in the Guild of Literature and Art.' As a result of his long friendship with the novelist and politician, Bulwer-Lytton, Dickens was always a welcome guest at Knebworth House and, it was during a visit in 1850, that the two men formulated their long-cherished plan to establish a Foundation, to assist improverished writers and artists of all kinds, and their dependants. As literary men themselves, they were only too aware of the precarious nature of their profession, and had witnessed at first hand, more than once, the dire straits to which some of their friends had been reduced.

Dickens, whose passion for the theatre was matched only by his genius as a writer, was at Knebworth on this occasion to give some performances of Ben Jonson's 'Every Man in his Humour', with a company which included Dickens himself, his wife and an array of distinguished friends. The performances, according to the inimitable Boz, went off '. . . in a whirl of triumph, and fired the whole length and breadth of Hertfordshire,' and the proceeds were donated to the Guild's funds.

During the following year, 1851, Bulwer-Lytton's play, 'Not so Bad as we Seem', was performed in London and the provinces. Once again, Dickens was in the Company of actors, and all proceeds were used to swell the Guild's coffers. After fifteen years or so, during which period both men invested an enormous amount of time and energy in the project, their dream was about to be realized. Dickens travelled up from his home at Gad's Hill for the inauguration ceremony and, in his speech, he explained to the assembled guests – famous and not so famous writers and artists on one hand, and the cream of Hertfordshire 'Society' on the other – that the houses '. . . had been built in the Gothic style and erected out of Guild funds on land donated by the Master of Knebworth.'

Sadly, the scheme proved to be a dismal failure. Perhaps

Dickens and Bulwer-Lytton had simply miscalculated the degree of independence which flourished among the literary and artistic community; most of whose members certainly felt that Stevenage was too far removed from their more usual haunts in London. One writer, summing up the general feeling of his brethren, said that although the Guild of Literature and Art was '. . . paved with good intentions, the road to Stevenage appeared to them the road to extinction.'

Nevertheless, there was at least one positive outcome to this episode. While visiting Knebworth in 1861, to inspect building work on the Guild's houses, Dickens was introduced to the famous 'Hertfordshire Hermit', 'Mad' James Lucas, who lived at Elmwood House, Redcoats Green. Although he was a wealthy man, Lucas chose to live in abject squalor, and is reputed to have worn only an old blanket. He subsequently appeared as Mr Mopes in Dickens's Christmas story for 1861, called 'Tom Tiddler's Ground'. This was much to the annoyance, it must be said, of the 'Hertfordshire Hermit' himself, who wrote an irate letter to the press, complaining about the uncomplimentary characterization. Redcoats Green is believed to have been the original 'Tom Tiddler's Ground', set '. . . among the pleasant dales and trout-streams of a green English county.'

The houses built by the Guild of Literature and Art were eventually demolished, to make way for Stevenage New Town; an ignominious end, perhaps, to a noble intention and further proof, if it were needed, of the ephemeral nature of mere bricks and mortar. Dickens's novels, however, are made of stronger stuff, and wherever they are read in the world, carry with them – at least in small measure – a breath of the 'sweet and very wholesome air of Hertfordshire.'

# The Adventures of a Gentleman:

## Bulwer-Lytton at Knebworth House

Edward George Earle Lytton Bulwer inherited Knebworth House, the famous Tudor mansion a few miles south of Stevenage, on the death of his mother in 1843. He then took her maiden name, and thereafter became known to the world as Bulwer-Lytton. Prior to the publication of 'The Pickwick Papers' in 1837, by a certain young writer called Charles Dickens, Bulwer-Lytton had been arguably the most popular novelist of his day; but he harboured no grudge for the eclipse he suffered at the hands of Boz, and the two men were to become firm friends.

The Lytton family's connection with Knebworth began at the end of the fifteenth century, when Sir Robert Lytton built a mansion on the present site. Much of the property was demolished during the early 1800s, although a part of it was spared and largely rebuilt. It was only later, however, when Bulwer-Lytton inherited Knebworth House, that it took on the external appearance which makes it such a distinctive landmark today.

Bulwer-Lytton was born in London in 1803; the third son of a general, William Earl Bulwer, who died four years later. Thus it was his mother, Elizabeth Barbara, daughter of Richard Warburton Lytton, who was the great parental influence in his life.

Given his distinguished lineage, Bulwer-Lytton's early education was somewhat unconventional. Eschewing the major public schools, he went first to Dr Hooker's establishment at Rottingdean, and then to Mr Wallington's, at Ealing. While studying at the latter, he was encouraged – during his mid-teens – to publish his first volume of poems.

Convention asserted itself in 1822, however, when Bulwer-Lytton went up to Trinity College, Cambridge, although his arrival there coincided with a particularly unhappy period in his life. He had fallen in love, while he was at Ealing, with a girl whose father demanded that she should marry another man. The young lady, who fully reciprocated Bulwer-Lytton's feelings, died within a few years of her enforced marriage, and the future heir to Knebworth was inconsolable. It was an incident which, to some extent, overshadowed his life, and he was to recall it in more than one of his novels.

In 1827, Bulwer-Lytton met Rosina Doyle Wheeler, probably through his friend, Lady Caroline Lamb, whose home at Brocket Hall was only a short distance from Knebworth. Now twenty-four, he was just one of a number of young men who had come under 'Caro' Lamb's spell for a while. Even during the last sad years of her tragic and brief life, she would still occasionally rally to exert a magnetism and charm which, on her best days, few could equal or resist.

The marriage between Bulwer-Lytton and Rosina, however, proved to be a disastrous one. His mother disapproved of the match so strongly that she terminated her son's allowance, and the couple were dependent on Bulwer-Lytton's income from writing as their only means of support. They had two children, before eventually separating in 1836. For whatever reason, their love had turned to loathing, certainly on Rosina's part, and she reappeared periodically over the years, sometimes causing embarrassing scenes by hurling insults at her estranged husband in public.

By the time he inherited Knebworth House, Bulwer-Lytton was both a popular writer and an established politician. His first success, 'Pelham, or the Adventures of a Gentleman', had been published in 1828 and was partly based on the true story of a murder which had taken place at Gill's Hill, near Elstree, five years earlier. 'Pelham' was followed by 'The Disowned' later the same year, and 'Devereux' in 1829. His reputation was such that he was able to command very high fees indeed: £1,500, for example, in the case of 'Devereux' and, later, when a cheap edition of his books was published, he was offered £20,000 – an enormous sum in those days – for the sale of the ten-year copyright.

Inevitably, some of Bulwer-Lytton's novels were more popular than others but one of his great successes, which appeared in 1834, was the historical romance, 'The Last Days of Pompeii'. Written after a visit to Italy it is, perhaps, the book for which he is best remembered today.

In 1831, Bulwer-Lytton became Member of Parliament for St. Ives. However, when his constituency disappeared with the passing of the Reform Bill the following year, he became the Member for Lincoln, and retained the seat until his resignation in 1841. It was to be eleven years before he sat in the House of Commons again. Disraeli persuaded him, during a visit to Knebworth House, to stand in the General Election of 1852, and Bulwer-Lytton was duly returned as the Tory Member for Hertfordshire. He was also briefly, from 1858–59, Secretary of State for the Colonies. At the election held prior to his appointment, Rosina had appeared on the hustings at Hertford to berate him in front of the crowds.

Before the death of his mother, Bulwer-Lytton had lived mainly in London. When he inherited Knebworth House, however, he spent most of his time – when he was not travelling abroad – in Hertfordshire. The secluded mansion, set deep in a wooded estate, suited him ideally as a place where he could write in peace, wholly untroubled by outside distractions. A spate of novels, including 'The Last of the Barons', 'Lucretia', 'Harold, the Last of the Saxons' and 'The Caxtons', together with a large-scale poetical work, 'King Arthur', were all completed between 1843 and 1850.

*Knebworth House, the distinctive home of Edward Bulwer-Lytton. (Photo: by kind permission of Lytton Enterprises Ltd.)*

Soon after inheriting Knebworth House, Bulwer-Lytton initiated extensive alterations, in keeping with his own taste for the Victorian Gothic style of architecture. With the help of sundry experts, he transformed the house both inside and out. The rather idiosyncratic features with which he adorned the exterior – comprising what at first glance appears to be a forest of turrets and domes, rising out of an undergrowth of battlements – are a wondrous if somewhat incongruous sight amid the gentle contours of Hertfordshire.

Bulwer-Lytton numbered many famous writers, artists and actors among his close friends, and it was not long before Knebworth House took its place in the literary and artistic life of the mid-nineteenth century. He was also a member of an exclusive dining-group, called 'The Portwiners'; an intimate circle which included Dickens, John Forster, the artists Edwin Landseer and Daniel Maclise, and the actor-manager, William Charles Macready. Macready, who lived for many years at 'Elm Place', Elstree, was the greatest tragedian of his day. At the end of the 1830s, he appeared – at Covent Garden – in several plays specially written for him by Bulwer-Lytton, including the comedy, 'Money', and the collaboration between the two men was a great success.

Perhaps the most enduring of Bulwer-Lytton's friendships was with Charles Dickens. They had met during the 1830s, at the beginning of Dickens's literary career, and Bulwer-Lytton had been able to introduce the ambitious younger author to some influential contacts. Out of their long friendship came the idea of forming the Guild of Literature and Art which, as we have seen, proved to be rather a dismal failure in the end despite all its good intentions. But the two men had a tremendous respect for each other's work; to such an extent, in fact, that Dickens – notoriously dogmatic when it came to his own writing, and editing the contributions of others for his various publications – allowed Bulwer-Lytton to persuade him to change the original ending of 'Great Expectations', and to provide a happy conclusion for Pip and Estella in the final paragraph of the novel. Bulwer-Lytton, said Dickens, 'supported his view with such good reasons that I resolved to make the change . . . and I have no doubt the story will be more acceptable through the alteration.'

On May 22nd 1847, the front cover of the periodical, 'Reynold's Miscellany', was devoted to a picture of England's three most popular writers of the day. They were Harrison Ainsworth, Bulwer-Lytton and Charles Dickens. Dickens, of course, is still as popular as ever; and a writer whose work has proved to be tailor-made for television and the cinema, thus guaranteeing him a modern audience. Ainsworth and Bulwer-Lytton, on the other hand, have been much less successful in maintaining their appeal for present-day readers. Bulwer-Lytton continued writing until his death in 1873 and, in his final novel, 'Kenelm Chillingly', completed during the last weeks of his life, his portrait of Lily Mordaunt was inspired by the ever-potent force of his lost love, fifty years earlier.

Although his work is now out of fashion, Bulwer-Lytton made a significant contribution to nineteenth-century literature. He was not only an immensely successful novelist, but also a poet, a playwright and a prolific journalist. He was created a Baronet in 1838, and raised to the Peerage in 1866 (at the end of his political career), as Lord Lytton, the 1st Baron Lytton of Knebworth. Charles Dickens, his close friend for more than thirty years, described him as '. . . a very great man, whose connection with Hertfordshire every other county in England will envy.'

*The Lytton Arms, Old Knebworth. A reminder of the family's local importance.*

# Lady Caroline Lamb:

# The Mistress of Brocket Hall

Lady Caroline Lamb's assessment of Lord Byron, that he was 'mad, bad and dangerous to know' was, it has to be acknowledged, a classic case of the pot calling the kettle black. Caroline Ponsonby, daughter of the third Earl of Bessborough, had shown herself to be – if not exactly a wayward – then certainly a difficult child almost from her birth, in November 1785.

Caroline was sent to Italy at the age of three after her mother, the former Lady Henrietta Spencer, had suffered a slight stroke. When she returned to England six years later, she was brought up by her grandmother, in the elegant and privileged surroundings of Devonshire House, Piccadilly. Before long, however, Lady Spencer had become so concerned about her granddaughter's eccentric behaviour and mercurial temperament, that she consulted a specialist in nervous disorders. His advice, as it turned out, could hardly have been less helpful in the circumstances. Caroline, he believed, should be handled with great care and discretion and, to all intents and purposes, be allowed to go her own way!

Throughout her life, Caroline Lamb was unpredictable and unstable, careering between bouts of unnatural gaiety on the one hand and fits of deep depression on the other, and leaving in her wake a trail of human debris; most notably in the person of her long-suffering and loving husband, William Lamb. Later, as Lord Melbourne – and after his wife's death – he became the young Queen Victoria's Prime Minister and a most trusted adviser.

Nowadays, Brocket Hall at Lemsford, near Welwyn, is a conference centre; a far cry from those days in the early nineteenth century when there was a racecourse at Brocket Park, and the Brocket Cup was a great event in the racing year. The original house, built by Sir John Brocket, dated from Tudor times, but it was demolished during the mid-eighteenth century, and replaced by the present building when Sir Matthew Lamb bought the estate, in 1746. It was to this palatial residence, with its gardens landscaped by 'Capability' Brown, that twenty-six year-old William Lamb brought his nineteen year-old wife, Caroline, for their honeymoon, in June 1805.

*Brocket Hall, Lemsford. (Photo: by kind permission of the Rt. Hon. Lord Brocket).*

The couple had first met at Brocket Hall when Caroline was only thirteen, and visiting the house in which William Lamb had spent much of his childhood. Six years later, after his elder brother, Peniston, had died, thus leaving William heir to the family title and fortune, they married. Had William remained in the position of second son, it is highly unlikely that the Duke of Bessborough would have been so much in favour of the match.

The Lambs' wedding-day was briefly overshadowed by one of Caroline's tantrums; an outburst which provided William with a fair example of what he could expect to endure over the next twenty years or so. For no obvious reason, and to the astonishment of the bridegroom and the distinguished congregation, she succumbed to a fit of hysteria; shouting at the bishop who was conducting the service and ripping her wedding-dress, before collapsing in a hysterical swoon.

What Caroline Lamb lacked in physical stature – she was short and of a slight build – she repaid in ample measure with the emotional havoc that she wreaked upon those closest to her. William, who remained a loyal and devoted husband almost until the end of her relatively brief life, could have experienced only fleeting moments of peace and happiness with her.

The birth of their only child, in August 1807, might in other circumstances have given William some comfort, and even hope for the future; but the boy, Augustus, was mentally handicapped, and only succeeded in adding to William's already crushing burden. His isolation was rendered ever more poignant by Caroline's inability to accept the situation. Never able to confront reality head-on, she lived in daily expectation of their son's condition improving, when there was manifestly no hope of it ever doing so.

The married life of the Lambs might easily have meandered on without attracting any great public attention, were it not for the events of 1812. The poet, Byron, had become something of an overnight sensation with the publication of the first two cantos of 'Childe Harold'. After reading the poem herself, Caroline could not rest until she had met its author and, eventually, an introduction was arranged at the London home of Lady Holland, in March. Within a few weeks, Caroline and

Byron had embarked upon a liaison that was as brief as it was turbulent and passionate.

Despite their intense attraction towards each other, however, their personalities and temperaments clashed violently, and it could only be a matter of time before the relationship foundered. By November, Byron was making it clear to his close friends that his connection with 'Caro' had ended; a state of affairs to which she responded in typical high dudgeon, by threatening some form of revenge upon him.

In the event, her response was rather more melodramatic than malicious. She gathered up some of the local village girls from Welwyn, dressed them in white, lit a bonfire and burnt copies – whilst retaining the originals! – of the letters Byron had written to her. The girls danced around the fire, chanting some lines that Caroline had written especially for the occasion.

'Ah, look not thus on me, so grave, so sad,'
the verse concluded,

'Shake not your heads, nor say the lady's mad.'

Byron left England in 1816, no doubt breathing a sigh of relief at leaving behind Lady Caroline Lamb who, since the end of their affair four years earlier, had continued to be a source of almost constant irritation. In May of the same year Caroline's first novel, 'Glenarvon', was published. Written at Brocket Hall, at great speed by candlelight, and without William's – or indeed anyone's – knowledge, it contained biting and transparent attacks on a number of the people closest to her, including her mother-in-law and her husband. The eponymous, colourful hero was based, perhaps inevitably, on Byron.

Byron, now removed from Caroline Lamb's presence by large tracts of land and sea, was untouched by the publication of 'Glenarvon' but, for William, the book was a final humiliation, and he insisted upon a Deed of Separation. Unpredictable as ever, Caroline persuaded her husband to agree to a reconciliation at the last moment, on the very day that lawyers arrived at Brocket Hall to obtain signatures for the document.

Caroline Lamb published two further novels. 'Graham Hamilton' appeared in 1822 and 'Ada Reis' the following year. Both of these were written with William's knowledge and co-operation, but neither met with the great success – or notoriety! – enjoyed by 'Glenarvon'.

After the final break with Byron, Caroline spent much of her time at Brocket Hall. Like William, she loved the place, and the peace she found on their Hertfordshire estate held a greater attraction than anything London 'Society' had to offer; which was fortunate, because she was increasingly unwelcome in that milieu. Years of outrageous behaviour, overlaid by the furore following the publication of her first novel, were at last having their effect.

However, all was far from well at Brocket. William came and went, immersing himself in politics and anything else that would serve to remove him from his wife's presence, while Caroline – whose health was steadily deteriorating, and certainly not being improved by large doses of laudanum and brandy – was creating havoc below stairs at Brocket Hall. Some of the older, more established servants, including the butler, Hagard, by all accounts, were able to turn a blind eye to their mistress's vagaries, but new recruits to the household staff were less tolerant, and quickly went in search of positions elsewhere.

When Byron died at Missolonghi in April 1824, Caroline Lamb was devastated by the news, and she bitterly regretted the later animosity which had existed between them when he left England in 1816, never to return alive. A cruel stroke of Fate was to follow in June when, walking with William near the gates of Brocket Park, she saw an impressive funeral procession making its way along the Great North Road, close to the estate; and learned that the cortege was carrying Byron's remains to the family vault at Hucknall Torkard church, near Newstead Abbey.

The decline in 'Caro's' health accelerated after Byron's death. Patient and supportive towards her until almost the very end, William finally insisted upon another Deed of Separation, which was put into effect during the summer of 1825. Caroline agreed to leave Brocket, although with great regret.

> 'Without a friend, without a home,
> I sit beneath my favourite tree.'

she wrote somewhat melodramatically, while waiting to depart.

Arrangements had been made for Caroline to live in a small house in London, but she was back at Brocket Hall before long; although with only her father-in-law for company as William had decided to move elsewhere. By the autumn of 1827, however, she was critically ill with dropsy and, by Christmas, it was clear that she was dying. Caroline asked to see her husband, who was then living in Ireland, declaring that he was the only person who had remained true to her. William rushed back to Brocket Hall, where he spent several days at Caroline's bedside, before she died – at the age of forty-three – on 26th January 1828. She was buried in Hatfield churchyard.

*Hatfield churchyard, the final resting-place of Caroline Lamb – and Mr Lirriper! The building beyond was formerly 'The Salisbury Arms', at the top of Fore Street.*

# Charles Lamb:

## Elia in Hertfordshire

Charles Lamb is best remembered today, perhaps, for 'Tales from Shakespeare', a book he wrote in collaboration with his sister, Mary. He was also a prolific essayist, poet and critic, and a Londoner to his very finger-tips. It was only occasionally, and usually with the greatest reluctance on his part, that he could be prized away from the capital, to visit any literary friends who were either foolhardy or inconsiderate enough to live in the country. However, as Edward Thomas has noted, Lamb was 'a good Hertfordshire man too, a lover of pure, gentle country – cornland, copse and water – and of gardens refined out of it.'

It is sometimes hard to reconcile this picture with what Lamb himself wrote in letters to his friends. 'A mob of happy faces crowding up at the pit-door of Drury Lane Theatre just at the hour of five,' he declared, in 1802, 'gives me ten thousand finer pleasures than I ever received from all the flocks of silly sheep.' Two years earlier he had written to the same friend, about his feelings for 'enchanting London, whose dirtiest drab-frequented alley I would not exchange for Skiddaw or Helvellyn.'

Charles Lamb was born in 1775 at Crown Office Row, in the Temple, where his father was employed as the clerk to Samuel Salt, a lawyer of the Inner Temple. He was educated at the charity Blue-Coat school, Christ's Hospital, after which he obtained an appointment at South Sea House, moving on to East India House in 1792. There he remained through many vicissitudes and despite a flourishing literary career, until 1825.

For much of his life Lamb lived in the very heart of London and, after their parents died, he cared for his sister, Mary, to whom he was devoted. She suffered from bouts of severe mental disorder and, during a fit of insanity in 1796, had attacked and killed her mother. Saved from a charge of manslaughter, she was committed to a private asylum for a while, at her brother's expense. Later, Charles assumed responsibility for her, and they shared a home together until Charles died in 1834.

The Lambs lived, at various times, in the Temple, Holborn and Covent Garden, before eventually moving out to 'the country margin of London' at Colebrooke Row, Islington, in 1823. Afterwards, they ventured further north to the more rural Enfield and, finally, to Edmonton, but the attractions of central London were always comfortably close at hand.

Lamb relished the life of literary London, enjoying the company of Wordsworth and Coleridge, Keats, William Hazlitt and others. He wrote sonnets and poems, including 'The Old Familiar Faces', which has a much-deserved place in the 'New Oxford Book of English Verse'. His classic work, 'Tales from Shakespeare', a joint effort with Mary, published in 1807, was designed to make Shakespeare's plays accessible to children, by re-telling them simply as stories, and it has remained a popular book ever since.

Mary also wrote a great deal on her own account, and Charles regularly contributed essays and criticism to 'The London Magazine' and other leading periodicals which flourished at the time. Like many of his literary contemporaries, in those far-off days before telephones and fax-machines, he vastly enjoyed writing letters, and these reveal much about Lamb and the circles in which he moved.

There was, however, an undercurrent in Charles Lamb's life, which occasionally rose to the surface not only in his correspondence, but in several essays and some of his poetry, too. His mother, Elizabeth, came from Hertfordshire. She was born at Hitchin where her own other, Mary Field, had been married in 1736. Mary's sister, Anne, had married into a family called Gladman and, when Charles and Mary Lamb were children, they had visited their Great Aunt Anne. She lived at Mackerye End, '. . . or Mackarel End, as it is spelt, perhaps more properly, in some old maps of Hertfordshire; a farm-house delightfully situated within a gentle walk from Wheathampstead,' as Lamb described it in his 'Essays of Elia'.

*Mackerye End, in 1991. (Photo: by kind permission of the present owner.)*

Mary Field, the Lambs' maternal grandmother, was also still living in Hertfordshire at this time. After the death of her husband, Edward, in 1766, she was employed as the caretaker of Blakesware, a manor house near Widford, which was the home of the Plumer family. Charles Lamb describes the house, in his essay 'Blakesmoor in H. . .shire', with its marble busts of

Roman Caesars in the hall, and Hogarth prints on the walls; all of which had made a great impression on his youthful mind.

In 1799, after re-visiting the house, (although Mary Field was dead by this time), he wrote to his friend, Robert Southey, that he could tell '. . . of an old house with a tapestry bedroom, the 'Judgement of Solomon' comprising one panel; I could tell of a wilderness and of a village church, and where the bones of my honoured grandam lie; but there are feelings which refuse to be translated.' Visits to the manor house and the environs of Widford inspired some of Lamb's early sonnets. In a later essay he wrote about Alice W. . .n, who was almost certainly Anne Simmons, a girl he had met at Blakesware, and with whom he had fallen in love at an early age.

Perhaps Charles Lamb's most tangible connection with Hertfordshire was established in 1812, when he inherited from his grandfather, Francis Field, a cottage delightfully named Button Snap, and situated at Cherry Green, near Westmill. It was the first – and only – property that he ever owned. It had a thatched roof and consisted of four rooms, a barn and almost three-quarters of an acre of land. The origin of the name is somewhat obscure, although Reginald Hine, in his definitive book, 'Lamb and his Hertfordshire', suggests that it is possibly a corruption of 'Buryton's Knapp', '. . . after the knap or knoll on which the cottage stands, close to the traces of an ancient moat surrounding the old Bury (or manor, or manor house), of the DeJany family of Westmill Green.'

Sadly, Charles Lamb never lived at Button Snap; it was occupied by a tenant – a Mr Sargus – to whom Lamb gave notice in February 1815 that he had parted with it. 'The rent that was due at Michaelmas,' he wrote, 'I do not wish you to pay me. I forgive it you as you may have been at some expenses in repairs.' Lamb sold the cottage for £50.

In later life Charles Lamb re-visited – both in fact and in fancy – those parts of Hertfordshire which he had first known as a child. In his letters and essays he described the memories and emotions that these re-explorations evoked. In 'Dream Children: A Reverie', for example, he recalls his love for Anne Simmons, with whom he had once declared himself, in an early sonnet,

'. . . well content to play
With thy free tresses all a summer's day
Losing the time beneath the greenwood's shade.'

In 'Blakesmoor in H. . .shire', he wanders over the remains of the old manor house, where '. . . in the cheerful store-room. . . I used to sit and read Cowley,' he recalls, 'and the hum and flappings of that one solitary wasp that ever haunted it about me – it is in mine ears now, as oft as summer returns.'

Perhaps, after all, his fondest memories of Hertfordshire centred around his childhood visits to Mackerye End, where Great Aunt Anne lived with her yeoman husband, James Gladman. After James's death in 1769, Anne stayed at the farm as housekeeper to Thomas Hawkins, until she died in 1799.

In 'Mackerye End in Hertfordshire', Lamb describes how he is possessed by a deep sense of nostalgia when visiting the house again after an absence of forty years. 'The sight of the old farm-house,' he wrote, 'though every trace of it was effaced from my recollection, affected me with a pleasure which I had not experienced for many a year.' Mary Lamb lovingly recalled those childhood days, too, in her collection of stories, 'Mrs Leicester's School', to which Charles also contributed.

Although it was in the rural setting of Church Street, Edmonton, that Charles Lamb died in 1834, he never truly left London, and Enfield was the furthest that he ever moved from the centre of it. 'A sweeter spot is not in the ten counties round,' he declared, 'than the willow and lavender plantations at the south corner of Northaw church.' Essentially it was a sense of nostalgia that the countryside held for him; he had no great desire to actually live in it. Nevertheless, despite his life-long attachment to London, 'hearty, homely, loving Hertfordshire' was a source of great pleasure and some inspiration to him.

# Robert Bloomfield:

## A Pastoral Poet at Shefford

Most visitors to the churchyard at Campton, a mile or so from Shefford, will be familiar with the name of Robert Bloomfield, but few will know – much less have read – his long poem, 'The Farmer's Boy'. Prior to 1966, when pupils from a Suffolk school made a pilgrimage to Bedfordshire, to clean up the inscription on his gravestone, few would have been able to read that either! 'Let his wild native wood notes tell the rest,' it proclaims, after giving the dates of his birth and death.

Although it is cast in similar mould to John Clare's 'Shepherd's Calendar' and James Thomson's 'The Seasons', Bloomfield's poem has probably fared the least well of the three in terms of the modern reader. And yet, when it was published in 1800 it met with enormous success. Almost 30,000 copies were sold within three years of publication, and it was translated into several languages, including Japanese. Its popularity turned Robert Bloomfield from a poor London shoemaker, scraping together a living at Bell-Alley, off Coleman Street in the City, into a famous and – that most rare species –

a prosperous poet, almost overnight.

Suddenly, Bloomfield was a celebrity, courted by the rich and famous, and catapulted from obscurity into the house of the Duke of Grafton in Piccadilly, and into the presence of the Prince of Wales himself. Other successes quickly followed: 'Rural Tales', 'Good Tidings or News from the Farm' and 'Wild Flowers' were all published by 1806, in a creative burst that, in terms of its financial success, would never be repeated throughout the rest of his life. As a result, Bloomfield was able to leave the cramped conditions of Bell-Alley and move with his wife, Mary-Anne, and their young family, to a comfortable house in the City Road, at that time on the edge of London in rural Islington.

Robert Bloomfield – a tailor's son rather than 'a farmer's boy' – was born at Honington, Suffolk, in December 1766. He was the youngest of six children, and far from strong. When his father died of smallpox, and his mother married again – producing, in time, another family of six – Robert was sent, at seven years of age, to his uncle's farm at nearby Sapiston. He was neither sufficiently strong nor old enough to work as a proper farm-labourer, and so he acted as a general dogsbody, fetching and carrying as required. Later, he was packed off to London, in the care of his two older brothers: George, a shoemaker and Nat, who had followed their father into the tailoring trade. Between them, they fed, clothed and generally looked after him.

George Bloomfield taught his young brother to be a shoemaker like himself and, it was during this period, while he was living and working in a garret at Pilcher's Court, off Bell-Alley, that Robert learned to read and write. He taught himself slowly and methodically, with the aid of old newspapers and a cheap dictionary. By the age of seventeen, he was already writing poetry, and he submitted one of his first efforts, 'The Village Girl', to 'The London Magazine'. It was accepted immediately, and Robert Bloomfield's fate as 'The Pastoral Poet' was decided.

Bloomfield and his family moved to Shefford in 1812. He had been considering the need to live more economically in the country, for some time. 'I have nothing to boast of as to health and appetite,' he had written to a friend, in 1811. 'I want to get well under a hedge, and cannot find one to my liking . . .'

The success of 'The Farmer's Boy' had inevitably brought Bloomfield into contact with many people over the years who admired his work. Patronized on the one hand by the Duke of Grafton and his circle, one of Bloomfield's less elevated – although no less ardent – admirers was a Shefford grocer, called Joseph Weston; a man who '. . . has read and thought more than any man I have ever found in his station of life . . .' wrote Bloomfield. Mr Weston had recently bought a house at Bedford Street – now called North Bridge Street – and the poet rented it from him. 'I live here for £15 per year rent,' he exclaimed in obvious relief, shortly after moving there in April 1812. '. . . In London I paid £40. The present Duke of Grafton continues his donation, so that I live rent free.'

*Robert Bloomfield's house at Shefford has now been converted into business premises.*

It was indeed fortunate that Bloomfield received such patronage, because 1812 proved to be a disastrous year for him financially. By September, his publisher had been declared bankrupt depriving him, as a result, of about £2,000; a huge sum of money, that he had been expecting in lieu of his copyrights.

Robert Bloomfield was in his mid-forties when he arrived at Shefford, with his greatest success as a poet behind him, and his health steadily eroded by money worries. What little capital he possessed was constantly being reduced still further. Not only had his publisher failed, but the calls on his purse were legion. His numerous brothers and sisters, and their children, at home in Suffolk, looked to him – as the great success of the family – whenever they needed financial assistance, and Bloomfield's heart was too soft to refuse them.

Despite these difficulties, however, Bloomfield's early days at Shefford were generally happy ones. 'We have a good house,' he enthused, 'a middling garden, and a rich country on all sides; every charm of spring surrounds us . . . the cuckoo plies his two notes all day, and a colony of frogs their one by night.' He amused himself locally; taking a glass of ale occasionally at 'The Green Man', or going to the theatre, when a band of strolling players performed in the malt-house at 'The King's Arms', nearby. 'My travels here are of a humble kind,' he informed a friend, '. . . seldom exceeding a nutting expedition or a gossip at the neighbouring farms.'

Retirement from London, however, did not mean that Bloomfield had given up work; far from it. He continued to write throughout the eleven years he lived at Shefford, but success on the scale of 'The Farmer's Boy', or anything approaching it, was not to come his way again. He branched out from poetry – although he did not abandon it – and wrote some children's stories. 'The History of Little Davy's New Hat' appeared in 1815, and was soon followed by 'The History of the Chicken and the Horse'. In 1822, his verse-tale, 'May-Day with the Muses' was published, and he also wrote a play – his only attempt at drama – called 'Hazlewood Hall', which appeared in 1823, just before his death.

Sadly, however, Robert Bloomfield was increasingly beset by tribulations of one kind or another. In 1814 his daughter, Mary, died at the age of twenty-one, and his wife became a religious fanatic; a close follower of Joanna Southcott from Devon. Mrs Bloomfield died with her mental faculties impaired, at Bedford Asylum in 1834; outliving her husband by eleven years. While Robert was still alive, however, she ran up such great debts with the local tradespeople that, eventually, he could no longer face leaving his own house; so ashamed was he of the predicament in which Mary-Anne had placed him.

At one stage, Bloomfield even contemplated leaving Shefford altogether, and moving back to London where his daughter, Charlotte, had found employment as a milliner in Cavendish Square and Charles, his son, was teaching at Putney. Despite making a house-hunting trip to the capital in 1820, however, the vaguely-formed plan came to nothing.

By 1823, Bloomfield's health – both physical and mental – was deteriorating rapidly. His mind became confused, and he suffered from hallucinations. He was also going blind. 'Writing is to me harder than digging was forty years ago,' he told his brother, George, in February. Except for his small income from the Duke of Grafton, he had little money. His eldest daughter, Hannah, took care of him during the final months. 'It was terrible to listen to him,' she recorded later. 'He was so depressed and nervously timid.'

Robert Bloomfield died, aged fifty-six, on 19th August 1823. 'Let me be buried anywhere but in a crowd,' he had asked, and he was laid to rest in the tiny churchyard at Campton, beneath a gravestone paid for by another good friend from Shefford, Thomas Inskip, who was later buried beside him.

*Campton church, and a part of the churchyard.*

Although they never met, Bloomfield and John Clare were great admirers of each other's work; their 'peasant' origins, after all, were not so dissimilar. After Bloomfield's death, Clare considered writing a biography of him, '. . . but I can hear nothing further than his dying neglected,' he noted in his diary, 'so it's of no use enquiring . . . for we know that to be the common lot of genius.' It was a singularly prophetic observation from one who was himself destined to die similarly neglected in the Asylum at Northampton, forty years later.

*Bloomfield's gravestone.*

# Loose Ends (2)

## Charles Abbot

Charles Abbot was a schoolmaster at Bedford, where he was also curate of St. Mary's and, for a time, St. Paul's. In addition he held the livings at Oakley and Goldington, but he is remembered today for an entirely different reason. In 1798, Abbot published his 'Flora Bedfordiensis', a pioneering botanical work, and only the third county flora of its type to appear; following hard on the heels of Oxfordshire and Cambridgeshire. 'Flora Bedfordiensis', which lists over thirteen hundred flowering plants, ferns, mosses and fungi, was the result of years of painstaking research undertaken by Abbot after he arrived at Bedford, from New College, Oxford, in 1788.

Abbot, who was born in 1761, published little else of interest beyond 'Hymns Composed for the Use of St. Mary's Church, Bedford' in 1791, and a handful of poems and sermons, but his magnum opus on Bedfordshire's flora secured his reputation as an important botanist. He died at Bedford in 1817.

## Rev. John Brown

The Rev. John Brown was the author of almost fifty books mainly about history and religion, but it is the biography, 'John Bunyan, His Life, Times and Work', for which he is primarily remembered today. Published in 1885, after twenty years' research, the book is widely regarded as the standard work on the subject, although Vera Brittain's 'In the Steps of John Bunyan', which appeared in 1950, has proved to be at least one worthy successor.

John Brown, a Lancashire man with Scots blood in his veins, came to Bedford in 1864, and stayed for forty years as Pastor of the Bunyan Meeting, living for most of that time at the Manse in Dame Alice Street. His output also included an important history of the Pilgrim Fathers, published in 1895, which further extended his reputation in America, where his great work on Bunyan earned him an honorary degree from Yale University. In 1911, Brown contributed sections on Bunyan and Andrew Marvell to the Cambridge History of English Literature.

When John Brown died in 1922 he was ninety-one; a similar age at which in 1950, his daughter, Florence Ada Keynes, published her autobiography, 'Gathering Up the Threads', which contains a delightful picture of life in Bedford during the years of her father's ministry there.

## Sir Richard Burton

There is some debate about Sir Richard Burton's place of birth. Some authorities favour Torquay, but we have the facts straight from the horse's mouth, Burton himself, writing in his autobiography, stated that he '. . . was born at 9.30pm 19th March 1821, at Barham House, Herts.'. Barham House – now demolished – stood in the parish of Elstree where, at the beginning of the following September, Burton was baptized in the local church; a fact which, in itself, lends credence to his Hertfordshire origins.

At best, however, Burton could have had only the vaguest recollection of Barham House (although, as a young man, a sense of nostalgia drove him back to look at the place), because he was whisked off to France and Italy by his parents, as an infant, to begin a lifetime of travel that would eventually take him to four continents.

Soldier, linguist and explorer extraordinary, Burton published over eighty books – at least half of which were travel volumes – including an account of his journey to the forbidden city of Mecca, which he visited disguised as a Moslem pilgrim.

Sir Richard Burton – he was knighted in 1886 – also published volumes of folklore and poetry, but it is for his highly-acclaimed, unexpurgated version of the 'Arabian Nights', which was a success both financially and with the critics when it appeared in 1885–8, that he is probably best remembered. Interest in his translations of 'The Kama Sutra' and 'The Perfumed Garden', originally published a few years before his death in 1890, was revived during the heady, eastern-oriented days of the late-1960s.

# William Godwin

Ware – home of the famous ten-foot square oak-carved Great Bed mentioned in Shakespeare's 'Twelfth Night' and Farquhar's 'The Recruiting Officer', and later conveyed to the Victoria and Albert Museum – was not only John Gilpin's unintended destination after his hazardous ride north from London. It was also the place where, during the late eighteenth century the writer and philosopher, William Godwin, underwent his great crisis of conscience. Twenty-one year-old Godwin arrived at the town in 1778 as a Congregational Minister. Within two years, however, he had departed, driven away by his loss of faith.

Little is known about Godwin's brief sojourn at Ware; although it must surely have been a profoundly difficult and unhappy time for him, as he attempted to fulfil his parish duties while wrestling with the religious doubts which assailed him. Before long, he had become a professed atheist with anarchical views, and had turned to writing as the means of earning his living.

Godwin's 'Enquiry Concerning Political Justice', published in 1793, turned him into one of the most famous and influential freethinkers of his day and his novel, 'Caleb Williams', was a great success when it appeared the following year. The involved plot, designed to highlight the iniquities of a society which rendered the poor weak and at the mercy of the rich and powerful, translated his political leanings into fiction.

Godwin married Mary Wollstonecraft – author of 'Vindication of the Rights of Woman' – in 1797, but the marriage was short-lived. She died later the same year after giving birth to their daughter, Mary: Shelley's future wife and famous in her own right as the author of 'Frankenstein'.

Despite his trials and tribulations, and the two tempestuous years at Ware, William Godwin lived to a ripe old-age. He died in 1836, aged eighty.

# Maria Edgeworth

Maria Edgeworth was a prolific writer for more than forty years, and gained an enviable reputation among her literary peers. Sir Walter Scott called her 'the great Maria' and the Russian novelist, Ivan Turgenev, claimed to have been considerably influenced by her novel, 'Castle Rackrent', which she published anonymously in 1800. Ruskin and Thackeray were among the many admirers of her work.

Maria Edgeworth was born in 1768 and, for a few years during her childhood, she spent holidays at a Georgian house in Northchurch, a mile or so west of Berkhamsted, where she stayed with her father and step-mother before returning to school each team at Derby. The family home, however, was in Edgeworthstown in County Longford, Eire, and it was there that she spent most of her life.

'Castle Rackrent', which is undoubtedly the most famous of Maria Edgeworth's novels, has a strong link with Hertfordshire. The character of Sir Kit Rackrent's English wife, who was kept locked up in her husband's Irish castle for seven years, is closely based on the unfortunate, real-life adventures of Lady Cathcart of Tewin whose fourth husband, Colonel McGuire – a fortune hunter of the most extreme sort – kept her incarcerated in appalling circumstances on his Irish estate for twenty years.

Lady Cathcart survived her long ordeal with amazing fortitude, and eventually returned to her old home at Tewin in 1764, after her husband had been killed in a duel. The indomitable spirit, which had served her so well during her imprisonment, never flagged. She enjoyed a long and vigorous old-age, and died just three years short of her hundredth birthday.

# William Cowper:

## The 'Stricken Deer' of Berkhamsted

The life of the poet, William Cowper, makes very sad reading indeed because, like John Clare a few generations later, his days were punctuated by recurring periods of mental illness. For a time, Clare had found comfort and healing under the gentle supervision of Dr Matthew Allen, in his asylum at High Beach on the margins of Epping Forest. Similarly, Cowper was fortunate to be placed in the care of Dr Nathaniel Cotton, whose 'Collegium Insanorum' was at St. Albans. In an age when the usual response to mental illness was exemplified by London's 'Bedlam' (the Bethlehem Hospital), where 'bleedings, vomits and chains' were the order of the day, both John Clare and William Cowper were lucky to meet with such enlightened physicians.

At this point, however, any further comparison between the two poets ends. Clare was the son of an agricultural labourer in Northamptonshire, and William Cowper was born – on 15th November 1731 – into one of Hertfordshire's leading families. His father, the Rev. John Cowper, had been rector of

Berkhamsted since 1722. He was also a chaplain to George II and a nephew of the Lord Chancellor, Earl Cowper. Despite their late eighteenth century grandeur, however, it was rumoured in the family, by all accounts, that the first Cowper, many generations earlier, had been an itinerant tradesman from Scotland, who had travelled out of the north carrying his own pack.

William's mother, Anne Donne, of Bedham Grange in Norfolk, whom John Cowper married in 1728, claimed descent from Henry III by several different lines, and another of her celebrated ancestors was the Metaphysical poet, John Donne. Anne gave birth to seven children, only two of whom – William and his brother, John – reached adulthood.

William spent his childhood in the old rectory at Berkhamsted, a house which he '. . . preferred to a palace.' Sadly, it has not survived into the twentieth century, to become the place of literary pilgrimage that it might otherwise have been. The Rev. John Croft, who was rector from 1810 to 1851, arranged for the old house to be demolished, and for a new rectory to be built just behind it.

*The Berkhamsted rectory of Cowper's childhood, from an 1850s drawing. (By kind permission of Berkhamsted & District Local History Society.)*

Looking back on his childhood in Berkhamsted, Cowper described it as a 'blissful time', but memory is notoriously selective, and there must have been many melancholy periods, in a house that witnessed – even by the standards of the day – more than its fair share of infant deaths. Then, in 1737, when William was only six, Anne herself died; a loss that dealt her young son a crippling blow. William idolized his mother. 'Everybody loved her,' he wrote later, 'and with an amiable character so impressed on all her features, everybody was sure to do so.'

William Cowper began his education, as a very young boy, at a small private school in Berkhamsted High Street, carried along by Robert ('Robin') Pope, the rectory gardener, in a

'. . . bauble-coach, and wrapped

In scarlet mantle warm and velvet cap.'

Shortly after his mother died, he spent a couple of months at Aldbury, under the supervision of the Rev. William Davis. But William's troubles began in earnest when John Cowper sent his rather timid and sensitive son to board at Dr Pitman's school, at Markyate Street (then known as Market Street), on the borders of Hertfordshire and Bedfordshire. Here, he was mercilessly bullied by a more senior pupil who was almost twice his age. Unaware of William's plight, his father kept him there for three years, before sending him on to Westminster School, where several previous generations of the Cowper family had been educated.

Westminster did much to bring William out of his shell, and he spent seven quite happy years there. He made some friends – with, amongst others, Warren Hastings, who was later to become the first Governor-General of British India – and found that he had a talent for games, particularly football and cricket. He developed an interest in literature, and discovered Homer. (Towards the end of his life, he published his own translations of 'The Iliad' and 'The Odyssey'.)

William left Westminster School in 1748, when he was seventeen, and returned to Berkhamsted. He stayed at home for nine months or so and fell in love with his cousin, Theodora Cowper. Although there was real affection between the pair, however, perhaps William's future was too uncertain or they were too young to actually contemplate marriage.

The onset of Cowper's prolonged bouts of depression and more serious mental disorders occurred after he moved to London at the beginning of the 1750s, when he was articled to a solicitor and later called to the Bar. 'The happiness of London,' said Dr Johnson, 'is not to be conceived of but by those who have been in it' and, as a young man, Cowper certainly found it an exhilarating city in which to live and work. As late as 1782, in a collection of his poems published that year, he styled himself as 'William Cowper Esq., of the Inner Temple'. But, by then, the country – first at Huntingdon and later at Olney, the place with which he is most closely identified – had been his natural refuge for many years.

The Rev. John Cowper died in 1756 and, with his father's death, William's connection with Berkhamsted virtually ceased. 'Then, and not till then,' he wrote, 'I felt that I and my native place were disunited for ever. I sighed a long adieu to fields and woods from which I once thought I should never be parted, and was at no time so sensible of their beauties as just when I left them all behind me.'

Seven years later, after experiencing several bouts of deep depression, Cowper suffered his first complete mental breakdown. His brother, John, immediately arranged for him to be placed under the supervision of Dr Nathaniel Cotton, whom William already knew slightly. Dr Cotton had acquired an enviable reputation for his humane treatment of the mentally ill, and it was to his establishment, called 'The College' or the 'Collegium Insanorum', on Dagnall Street, St. Albans, not far from the Abbey, that William was admitted on 7th December 1763.

William Cowper spent eighteen months at the 'Collegium Insanorum', during which time his condition fluctuated endlessly. Eventually, however, he responded to Nathaniel Cotton's method of treatment. 'I was not only treated by him with the utmost tenderness while I was ill, and attended with the utmost diligence,' he wrote later, 'but when my reason was restored to me, and I had so much need of a religious friend to converse with . . . I could hardly have found a fitter person for the purpose.'

In June 1765, Cowper was able to leave the 'Collegium Insanorum', accompanied by his servant, Sam Roberts, and a young boy called Dick Coleman, the son '. . . of a drunken cobbler at St. Albans.' He took lodgings in Huntingdon, where he could be discreetly supervised by his brother, John, who lived nearby in Cambridge. A few months later, William met the Rev. and Mrs Unwin and, in November, moved into their house. After the Rev. Unwin's death in 1767, Cowper and Mrs Unwin moved to Olney.

It was at Olney, in Buckinghamshire, that Cowper wrote many of his major pieces, including what is probably his best-known long poem, 'The Task'. It was also where he collaborated with the evangelical curate, John Newton, on 'Olney Hymns', which appeared in 1779 – one of Cowper's more famous contributions included 'God moves in a mysterious way' – and where he toiled away on his translation of Homer.

In a lighter vein, Cowper wrote 'The Diverting History of John Gilpin'. John Gilpin and his wife decided to celebrate their twentieth wedding anniversary by visiting 'The Bell' at Edmonton. Mrs Gilpin and her children, travelling in a chaise and pair arrive safely but, through lack of space, John is obliged to make his way there separately, riding on an unfamiliar horse. He loses control of the beast, and is taken on well into Hertfordshire.

'Stop, stop, John Gilpin! Here's the house,'
cries his family, as he speeds past 'The Bell'.
'The dinner waits and we are tired;'
Said Gilpin – 'So am I!'
But yet his horse was not a whit
Inclined to tarry there;
For why? – His owner had a house
Full ten miles off at Ware.'
This 'diverting history' was indeed a diversion for Cowper. It was written in 1782 at the suggestion of his friend, Lady Austen, during another bout of deep depression.

Despite several attempts at suicide during his long life, William Cowper died of natural causes on 25th April 1800, at East Dereham; by which time he had not visited Berkhamsted for over forty years. Writing in 1788 about his birthplace, he said that '. . . I might pass through a town in which I was once a principal figure, unknowing and unknown.' But his spirit still lingers in odd corners of Berkhamsted, and not least in the thirteenth-century parish church of St. Peter's. He was baptized there, on 13th December 1731. It is the church where his father preached, and where his mother and brothers and sisters are buried; and where the Cowper Memorial Window was installed in 1872, paid for out of funds raised by the Rev. John Cobb.

*St. Peter's church, Berkhamsted, as Cowper would have known it, from an early nineteenth century engraving. (By kind permission of Berkhamsted & District Local History Society.)*

119

# John Howard of Cardington:

## Portrait of a Prison Reformer

John Howard is remembered primarily as a prison-reformer and philanthropist, whose name was enshrined in the Howard League for Penal Reform. Yet, as a glance at the 'Oxford Companion to English Literature' will confirm, his crusading spirit turned him into a writer, too. His influential work, bearing its rather cumbersome title, 'The State of the Prisons in England and Wales, and an Account of Some Foreign Prisons and Hospitals', was published in 1777. The book established his credentials as an authority on prison conditions, and placed him firmly in the vanguard of attempts to reform the penal system.

It was an unlikely climax to a life which had begun somewhat inauspiciously at Hackney, in 1726. Born with a frail and delicate constitution, John Howard was the son of an upholsterer, who had his own business at Smithfield. Because of his uncertain health, however, and in the absence of his mother who died when he was only five, John spent much his childhood at Cardington, a couple of miles to the south-east of

Bedford, where his father owned some property. The young boy was nursed and taken care of by the wife of one of his father's tenants on the estate.

Seven years at Mr Worsley's school in Hertford were followed by a further two at Moorfield's Dissenting Academy in London, before John Howard was apprenticed, at the age of fifteen, to a wholesale grocer in the City. It was a trade which suited neither his health – the atmosphere in the warehouse affected his chest – nor his temperament. Thus, when his father died a year or so later, in 1740, John cancelled his indentures.

The delicate child grew into a sickly – although wealthy – young man; a martyr not only to consumptive tendencies, but to his nervous disposition as well. At twenty-seven, however, he married Sarah Lardeau, who was almost twice his age. She had been both his landlady and his nurse during several bouts of severe illness, and the pair had grown fond of each other. Sadly, the marriage – the ceremony took place during the autumn of 1753 – was short-lived, as Sarah died just two years later.

It was Sarah's death which led John Howard, indirectly, to the great work for which he is remembered. A severe earthquake shook Lisbon – causing over twenty thousand deaths – during the month in which Sarah died. In an attempt, perhaps, to assuage his grief, Howard set out to inspect the devastation at first-hand. However, the Portuguese boat on which he was travelling was captured by a French vessel, and Howard found himself thrown into prison. Initially he was held in a dungeon at Brest, where the conditions were unbelievably squalid. 'Perhaps what I suffered on this occasion,' he wrote later, in 'The State of the Prisons . . ' 'increased my sympathy with the unhappy people whose case is the subject of this book.'

When he finally returned to England, three months later, John Howard went immediately to the house which now bears his name at Cardington, determined to assume the responsibilities of a country landowner. He had a great affection for the place, '. . . a village of much neatness with all the houses so smart and the green nicely planted,' as John Byng recorded in his Diaries.

Cardington, in its more recent history, has become indelibly linked with the airship R101, which was not only built there but also set off from one of Cardington's vast grey-green hangars for its ill-fated maiden flight to India in 1930.

*Old airship hangars dominate the Cardington landscape.*

*Howard's House, at Cardington.*

In 1758, John Howard married again. On this occasion there was no discrepancy in age, and his wife was a distant relative: Henrietta Leeds of Croxton, in Cambridgeshire. Together, they set to work earnestly on the estate where – in anticipation of the great vogue for philanthropy, which would reach its peak in Victorian England – they did much not only to enhance the property itself, but also to improve the quality of life for their tenants.

Cottages which had been built on low ground liable to flooding, for example, were pulled down and re-built on drier land elsewhere. Each tenant was provided with a garden in which to grow vegetables, and elementary education – reading and needlework for the girls; reading, writing and arithmetic for the boys – was also introduced. An air of paternalism wafted over the estate, even if John Howard could sometimes be a strict father! He demanded hard work, respectful behaviour and sobriety from all his tenants, but as a landlord he was considerably in advance of his time.

John Howard's second marriage lasted only seven years; Henrietta died in 1765, a few days after giving birth to a son. 'John my son was born about four o'clock, March 27th,' Howard recorded dolefully. 'Sabbath evening, March 31st . . . died the dear mother.' Left once more on his own, Howard was in despair. He stayed on at Cardington for over a year but, leaving his son with a nurse, he finally resorted to travelling again to ease his sorrow. He journeyed to France and Holland, crossed the Alps, and spent a considerable time in Italy.

In 1771, he settled once more at Cardington from where, every Sunday, he walked the few miles to Bedford to attend church. He had a house built in Mill Street, where he allowed a family to live rent-free throughout the week, on condition that he was able to use the parlour for reflection and refreshment on Sundays.

The last – and most important – phase of John Howard's life, however, opened in 1772, when he was appointed High Sheriff of Bedfordshire. Regularly attending the assize court as a part of his official duties, Howard decided to investigate for himself the conditions in which prisoners existed at Bedford Gaol. He was horrified by what he found. Improperly fed and watered, housed in tiny cells, often without adequate light or ventilation, and with dirty straw for bedding, he was reminded of his own dreadful experience in France, many years earlier.

Among the numerous iniquities that Howard soon uncovered, was that gaolers themselves were not paid a salary, but earned their livelihood by fees exacted from the inmates. 'The distress of prisoners,' he noted, in the Introduction to his book, 'of which there are few who do not have some imperfect idea, came more immediately under my notice when I was sheriff of the county of Bedford, and the circumstance which excited me to activity in their behalf was the seeing some . . . after having been confined for months dragged back to gaol, and locked up again till they should pay sundry fees to the gaoler . . .'

Determined to rectify these injustices, Howard set out on a personal crusade, inspecting gaols not only throughout Britain, but abroad as well. Incredibly, between 1775 and 1790, despite enjoying far from robust health, he made seven large-scale journeys, covering in the process over forty-two thousand miles, and travelling entirely at his own expense. It was from the research gathered on the first two of these major expeditions, that he compiled the main body of his book, 'The State of the Prisons . . '

Some of John Howard's proposals – regarding British prisons, at least – were translated into legislation even before his book was published. In 1774, for example, after some of his evidence had been presented to a House of Commons Select Committee, the detention of prisoners solely on the grounds that they could not afford to pay gaolers' fees was outlawed. Some of the matters relating to sanitation and ventilation were also tackled, in an attempt to reduce the prevalence of the usually fatal gaol-fever, or typhus.

John Howard would retreat to the sanctuary of his house at Cardington between journeys, and put away for a while the vinegar-bottle which he habitually carried with him when visiting prisons, to ward off infection. Despite his other pressing concerns, he never failed in his obligations to his Bedfordshire estate, for which he was always devising improvement schemes. But Cardington was resonant with sad reflections too: associations with Henrietta, whose loss he always felt keenly, and with their son whose emotional health was so poor that, much to his father's distress, he was finally committed to an asylum.

At the beginning of 1790, John Howard embarked upon a trip to inspect prisons in Eastern Europe. During the previous year, he had published a second, smaller book, containing the research and recommendations drawn from more recent tours of inspection. Unfortunately, on this occasion, the good luck which had attended him throughout seventeen years of visiting foul-smelling, disease-ridden prisons ran out, and he succumbed to gaol-fever. Within only a short time of leaving Cardington he was dead.

John Wesley described Howard as '. . . one of the greatest men in Europe,' and it is a measure of his greatness, perhaps, that a statue of him in classical dress was the first memorial to be erected in St. Paul's Cathedral. On St. Paul's Square in Bedford, however, he cuts a rather more familiar figure, wearing the riding coat and boots that mark him out as the seasoned traveller which indeed he was. A salutary reminder, perhaps, that he died on his travels, on 20th January 1790, and that he lies buried near Kherson in the Ukraine, far from home.

# A Poet in the Pulpit:

# Edward Young at Welwyn

'Procrastination is the thief of time,' wrote Dr Edward Young, the poet-rector of Welwyn, although it has to be admitted that the quotation is considerably more famous than its author. Shakespeare, Milton or John Donne, perhaps, seem more likely candidates for the source of such a wise old saw; yet it was a line, tucked away among ten thousand or so others, in Young's 'The Complaint, or Night Thoughts on Life, Death and Immortality', which appeared in nine books from 1742-5.

Not widely read today, perhaps, this long rambling poem, largely inspired by the death of Young's wife, achieved great popularity in Britain and Europe, when it first appeared. It was translated into several languages, and went through almost two hundred editions in the United States of America in little more than a century. Robespierre, it is whispered, slept with a copy of it under his pillow during the French Revolution and the poem was an important contribution to the 'Graveyard School': lengthy, reflective and usually melancholy pieces, which achieved a vogue during the eighteenth century. Gray's

'Elegy Written in a Country Churchyard' is probably one of the more famous examples of the genre.

When Dr Johnson came to prepare his 'Lives of the English Poets', he wrote that Edward Young, 'with all his defects . . . was a man of genius and a poet.' 'Night Thoughts' was without a doubt Young's most celebrated work, but he had also written a number of plays, which were produced with varying degrees of success at Drury Lane. His series of satires, 'The Universal Passion', had appeared from 1725–8.

A general lack of literary success, however, and a reluctance to employ the law degree which he had gained at Oxford, resulted in Young following his father into the Church. After serving for a brief period as chaplain to the newly-enthroned George II, he was presented to the living at Welwyn in 1730, when he was just a few years short of his fiftieth birthday. The post also carried with it the title of Lord of the Manor.

The Elizabethan rectory which was to be Edward Young's new home, stood in one of the most ancient corners of the village. A year after he moved to Welwyn, however, Young married Lady Elizabeth Lee, a daughter of the Earl of Lichfield. She was a widow with two children and – the rectory proving too cramped for their needs – Young rented a house called Guessens, which stands to this day in Codicote Road, opposite St. Mary's church. Much altered over the years, and extended during Dr Young's time, the house is of fifteenth or sixteenth century origin. Serving as the rectory in an unofficial capacity for virtually all of Young's thirty-five years' incumbency, Guessens had actually been a registered place of worship for non-conformists during the 1690s. Much later, in 1955, the property was purchased by Welwyn Evangelical Church for use as a manse and a men's hostel and, nowadays, it is home to the European Missionary Fellowship.

Given the theatre's dubious reputation during the eighteenth century, parsons – while often diarists and poets – were seldom playwrights, and in this respect Young was unusual. His first play, 'Busiris', had been produced at Drury Lane in 1719, when he was thirty-six and some years before he took Holy Orders. Young himself could not fail to be aware of the incompatibility of the two roles. When a production of his tragedy, 'The Brothers', coincided with his ordination, he withdrew the piece from the theatre, conscious no doubt of the equivocal nature of his position. The play was eventually performed at Drury Lane in 1753, however, while he was still rector of Welwyn.

*Guessens, in Codicote Road, Welwyn.*

Poet and playwright though he was, Edward Young was not an absentee vicar; a dilettante who left his parish in the hands of an overworked curate. Nevertheless, his official duties in eighteenth-century Welwyn, a sequestered village surrounded by fields and woodland, would have been less than onerous. When services were over and his parishioners ministered to, there was ample time left for writing and socializing, and for enjoying family life. Young's marriage, embarked upon in middle-age, was a singularly happy one, but sadly cut short by his wife's death in 1741.

Shortly afterwards, Young's step-daughter died of consumption, and this double blow crushed him for a while, although he was left with his own eight year-old son, Frederick, to comfort him. 'Night Thoughts', largely composed while he was riding through the Welwyn lanes on parish business, was a poet's response to these tragic losses. The poem, as its title suggests, is a reflection both on life's trials and immortality. Dr Johnson thought highly of it. 'Particular lines are not to be regarded,' he declared, 'the power is in the whole, and in the whole there is a magnificence of vast extent and endless diversity.'

By now, Edward Young was approaching sixty and already an elderly man by contemporary standards. For someone of his melancholic disposition, it would have been all-too easy to withdraw from the fray, and rest upon the laurels of 'Night Thoughts'. But he did not. He engaged a housekeeper, Mrs Hallows, and – if the idyllic nature of his first ten years at Welwyn could not be repeated – he nevertheless achieved a tolerable degree of content. Some of those people who knew him towards the end of his life, have claimed that Young became morose and increasingly withdrawn. Frederick told Dr Johnson many years later, that his father '. . . was too well-bred a man not to be cheerful in company; but he was gloomy when alone.'

Young found much to occupy him, however, beyond his mere parish duties. In 1749, he established St. Mary's School, for the education of sixteen Welwyn boys and, eleven years later, he formed a trust to guarantee its financial security after his death. He made arrangements for the restoration of St. Mary's church tower, which had collapsed in a fierce storm almost a century earlier. He was also a member of the Welwyn Turnpike Trust; a body which existed primarily to oversee the upkeep of public highways in an area from Lemsford to Hitchin, and from Welwyn to Stevenage and Biggleswade. Given that the Trust's main source of income was derived from tolls levied on road travellers, this was probably his least popular role!

Young was instrumental in one attempt, however, to place Welwyn firmly on the map. He rediscovered a chalybeate spring – whose existence had been known about centuries earlier, although lately forgotten – in the vicinity of Mill Lane. 'The waters here are not a new thing,' he told his friend, the novelist Samuel Richardson. 'They were in great vogue 50 years ago. But . . by degrees they were forgot.' The iron-rich properties of the spring were thought to be of excellent medicinal value, and highly likely to make Welwyn's fortune as a spa resort; spas – as Tunbridge Wells, Harrogate and Bath could amply testify – were favourite haunts of the ailing and fashionable during the eighteenth century.

In 1759, Edward Young built the Welwyn Assembly Rooms in Mill Lane which, for a time at least, served their turn as a meeting-place for those who came to take the waters. 'We have a physician, now near us, who drinks them himeself all winter,' Young reported in a letter to Richardson, 'and a lady comes seven miles every morning for the same purpose . . I do assure you,' he added, 'that this spring has every virtue of Tunbridge in it.'

In the end, however, Welwyn obstinately refused to join the ranks of the other great English spas. Although a steady flow of visitors came over a number of years during the season, chiefly because it was conveniently near London, Welwyn's popularity – such as it was – dwindled and, eventually, the Mill Lane Assembly Rooms were converted into a row of cottages. Edward Young, however, did not live to see that day. He died only six years after the Assembly Rooms had been erected.

*Old Assembly Rooms cottages, in Mill Lane, Welwyn.*

Towards the end of his life, Young became increasingly disgruntled by the fact that neither his literary nor his clerical achievements had gained him much – if any – advancement. Patronage, that system of support which had inked the nibs of many a literary pen in Young's day, seemed largely to have passed him by, and he had received no promotion in the Church.

'My very brother knows me not,

'I've been so long remembered I'm forgot,'

he wrote in 'Night Thoughts'. The lines seemed tailor-made for him. But in 1761, when he was approaching eighty, some form of recognition came with his appointment as 'clerk of the closet' to Augusta, the Princess Dowager of Wales. His last substantial poem, 'Resignation', was published the following year.

Edward Young died in 1765 at Guessens, the house which he had originally rented but now owned. It had been his home for more than thrity years. Most visitors to St. Mary's church nowadays, who pause before the memorial tablet to Dr Young placed by his son on the west wall, may not be immediately familiar either with his name or his achievements. Yet, in his day he was one of the best-known of English poets and considered a 'great man' by Dr Johnson.

# Pages from a Diary:

# Samuel Pepys in Hertfordshire

Samuel Pepys was a gregarious man, who enjoyed the companionable atmosphere of tavern and coffee-house alike, and who was much at home in that warren of seventeenth century political intrigue, the Palace of Whitehall. It was his ability to get on well with people, coupled with a natural aptitude and enthusiasm for his work, which led to his outstandingly successful career at the Admiralty; although the patronage of his relation, Sir Edward Montagu, was also a great asset.

Born in 1633, Samuel Pepys lived through some of the most turbulent years in England's history, from the outbreak of Civil War and the execution of Charles I during the 1640s, to the so-called 'glorious revolution' of 1688. His famous Diary, begun on 1st January 1660 and maintained continuously for almost a decade, covers the Restoration, the Plague and the Great Fire of London. As such, his first-hand accounts of these momentous events have made not only fascinating reading but also provided an invaluable primary source for historians, since the

Diary – written in an obscure system of shorthand – was first published in an abbreviated form in 1825.

Although Pepys was born and lived virtually all his life in London, the Diary has considerable Hertfordshire interest. Pepys came from fenland stock, and he traversed the county numerous times in the course of visiting his various relations in Huntingdonshire and Cambridgeshire.

An entry for 24th February 1660, made only weeks after the Diary was begun, is typical of many that were to follow over the next ten years or so. Setting off to spend a few days at Cambridge, where he was to meet his father and brother, Pepys and a travelling companion left London at 7am, '. . . the day and the way very foul . . At Puckeridge,' he reported, 'we had a loin of mutton fried.'

Therein lies part of the charm of Pepys's Diary; a closely written shorthand manuscript of about 3,000 sheet cataloguing, on the one hand, the great affairs of state as witnessed by a man close to the centre of events yet, on the other, liberally peppered with intimate personal details. The loin of mutton at Puckeridge, for example, was followed eighteen months later by 'a mouthful of pork . . ' at Baldock, 'which',

*Welwyn, where Pepys enjoyed a particularly good night's sleep in 1661, and where Edward Young was rector of St. Mary's from 1730-1765.*

Pepys indignantly pointed out, 'they made us pay 14d for . . ' As there was a local fair in progress at the time, he was possibly the victim of an unscrupulous salesman's temporarily inflated prices!

However, that particular day ended on a happier note. Pepys, who was on his way home – with his wife, Elizabeth – from Cambridgeshire, travelled by way of Stevenage to Welwyn, 'where we supped well,' he noted, 'and had two beds in the room, and so lay single, and still remember it that of all the nights that ever I slept in my life I never did pass a night with more epicurism of sleep.'

Elizabeth Pepys, who was not always the most robust of travelling companions for her husband, occasionally came to grief on the deeply rutted and often waterlogged roads of seventeenth-century Hertfordshire. She 'got a fall but no harm,' on the way to Ware, on 17th September 1661 and the following day, as Pepys recorded, 'my wife, in the very last dirty place of all,' near Puckeridge, 'got a fall, but no hurt, though some dirt.' In the rough-and-ready manner of the day, however, Elizabeth rode on seemingly undaunted and arrived at the house of Pepys's uncle in Cambridgeshire that evening, without further mishap.

Exactly two years later, poor Elizabeth was in the wars again, during a journey to another of her husband's relations, this time at Brampton, near Huntingdon. Riding without incident as far as Buntingford, Elizabeth dismounted there and drank some cold beer. She was hot with travelling and the cold drink disagreed with her, so that she was violently sick. A good night's sleep restored her, however, and she was able to continue her journey the next day without any ill-effects. Despite these minor setbacks, Pepys considered his wife '. . . a very good companion so long as she is well.'

Pepys's journeys through Hertfordshire were often accomplished in something of a hurry; he was a busy man, after all, with steadily increasing responsibilities and often pressing concerns at work. But he was an inquisitive man, too, and readily deflected by his appetite for fresh experiences. These were the characteristics, no doubt, which led him '. . . to see the Wells', during a visit to Barnet in July 1664, where he '. . . drank three glasses, and walked, and came back and drank two more.' An excess of mineral water was possibly the reason for that day's entry ending of a less vigorous note. '. . . Not being very well,' he wrote, 'I betimes to bed.'

*Elizabeth Pepys was taken ill at Buntingford.*

Nevertheless, he was not put off by the experience. After being detained in London more than usual during 1665 and 1666, on account of the Plague and the Great Fire, he returned to Barnet in August of the following year, where he paused at 'the Wells' to drink another three glasses of mineral water, before going on to the 'Red Lion', '. . . where we 'light, and went up into the Great Room, and there drank, and eat some of the best cheese-cakes that ever I eat in my life.'

Afterwards, Pepys rode on to Hatfield where – it being the 'Lord's day' – he, in company with his wife and sundry other travelling companions, attended church and 'bespoke dinner' at 'The Salisbury Arms', at the top of Fore Street, '. . . next my Lord Salisbury's house.' Hatfield House, built between 1607 and 1611 by Robert Cecil, 1st Earl of Salisbury, was a great favourite with Pepys. During a visit in 1661, he had '. . . met with Mr Looker, my Lord's gardener . . . who showed me the house, the chapel . . . and, above all, the gardens, such as I never saw in all my life, not so great flowers, nor so great gooseberries, as big as nutmegs.'

*St. Mary's, Baldock.*

On 7th October 1667, the Diary finds Pepys and his wife staying overnight at the 'Reindeer Inn', Bishop's Stortford, while on their way once more to Brampton. Four days later they rode home, by way of Stevenage and Barnet, carrying some bags of gold which Elizabeth and Pepys's father had buried in the latter's garden the previous June, during the threat of a Dutch invasion.

Pepys made the final entry in his Diary on 31st May 1669, in the belief that he was going blind. 'And this ends all that I shall ever be able to do with my own eyes in the keeping of my journal,' he reported, that day. Doubtless there were many more excursions into Hertfordshire, but we can know nothing of them in the absence of his intimate record, beyond the fact that Elizabeth would no longer have been his travelling companion. She died only four months after Pepys had written the last entry in his Diary.

Pepys was to live for another thirty-four years; years which – despite poor eyesight – saw his appointment as Secretary for Admiralty Affairs and his election as President of the Royal Society. After his death in 1703, the Diary was preserved at Magdalene College, Cambridge, where Pepys had been an undergraduate. John Smith, the man who deciphered the manuscript over one hundred years later, eventually became rector of St. Mary's church, Baldock, and thereby strengthened the link between the world's most famous diarist and Hertfordshire.

# John Bunyan:

# A Pilgrim in Bedfordshire

Matthew Arnold described John Bunyan – neither unkindly nor unfairly – as 'the Philistine of genius in literature'; for the 'Immortal Dreamer' was an uncultured – although not an unlettered – man, and most certainly an unlikely candidate as a best-selling author. Yet there have been few writers whose work could rival the success of 'The Pilgrim's Progress': a book which has been translated into more than two hundred languages and dialects, and which has sustained its influence and popularity for over three hundred years. It is an astonishing achievement by any standards – only worldwide sales of the Bible exceed those of Bunyan's masterpiece – and even more remarkable when measured against the author's humble origins in seventeenth-century Bedfordshire.

John Bunyan was born in 1628 at a cottage – long since demolished – which stood surrounded by low-lying fields between Elstow and Harrowden. Today a granite block, erected in 1951, marks the site which can be reached by a footpath. It is a spot which, during wet weather, renders the clayey mud underfoot such hard-going that comparisons with the 'Slough of Despond' immediately spring to mind.

*The commemorative stone, marking the site of John Bunyan's birthplace.*

'For my descent then,' Bunyan wrote later, 'it was of a low and inconsiderable generation, my father's house being of that rank that is meanest and most despised of all the families in the land.' His father, Thomas was, in fact, a comparatively well-off brazier or tinker: a man who mended pots, pans, kettles and larger metal objects in Elstow and the surrounding villages.

Bunyan was brought up to follow the same trade, although not before he had been sent to school where he learned to read and write. In one sense, these accomplishments will have marked him out at an early age. Both his father and grandfather were truly illiterate, and John's childhood was passed in an England where the notion of universal education, as we know it today, had not even been conceived much less executed. Happily, though, '. . . notwithstanding the meanness and inconsiderableness of my parents,' Bunyan tells us, 'it pleased God to put it into their hearts to put me to school to learn both to read and write, according to the rate of other poor men's children.'

The story of John Bunyan's life, so far as it is known, has been told many times and at great length elsewhere, but even an outline of his own progress from a humble – and, as he would insist, a blaspheming – tinker to the author of approaching sixty tracts and books, demonstrates a feat of unique proportions which, given the climate and circumstances of his time, almost beggars belief. We read how as a boy and a young man he played sports on the village-green at Elstow on Sundays; how he had a passion for dancing and bell-ringing, and a tendency to use bad language.

Entering adolescence in an England torn apart by Civil War, Bunyan enlisted in the Parliamentary army during the autumn of 1644. When he was demobilized about two years later, he returned to Elstow to resume life as a tinker and, before long, he was married and had moved to a cottage in the centre of the village itself.

*Elstow High Street, 1991.*

A subtle change was wrought on Bunyan after his marriage. The 'roaring-boy' mellowed and, although '. . . as poor as poor might be, not having so much household stuff as a dish or spoon betwixt us both,' Bunyan and his wife, Mary, now possessed two devotional books: 'The Plain Man's Pathway to Heaven' and 'The Practice of Piety', bequeathed to them by Mary's father, and the reading of which gave Bunyan much food for thought.

This proved to be the first of several steps along the road to Bunyan's conversion. He started going to church on Sundays; took much to heart a sermon, preached by the vicar of Elstow, on the habit of Sabbath-breaking; was suitably chastened, when reproved by a woman in the village for his vehement cursing and swearing, and he began to read the Bible and study the Ten Commandments.

Bell-ringing, dancing and sport were abandoned and, following his baptism in the Ouse at Duck Mill, Bunyan soon established himself as a popular and effective preacher, after joining the Independent church of St. John's, Bedford. Some of those people who were familiar with his background were sceptical, and still thought of him as a 'profane tinker'. By others he was called, a touch jokingly, 'Bishop' Bunyan. History, however, has proved to be a fairer and more reliable judge of the man, despite the air of martyrdom which twelve years in prison were likely to lend him.

As a Non-Conformist after the Restoration, preaching without a licence was a transportation – and ultimately a hanging – offence, although Bunyan evaded both of these extremes. Church-goers were required to attend services conducted by members of the ordained clergy, and the growing popularity of the Independent ministry was perceived as a threat to the established order. Towards the end of 1660, Bunyan – who was forced to preach in secret – was arrested for speaking at a large open-air meeting at Lower Samsell, near Harlington. For consistently refusing to renounce his Non-Conformist practices, he languished in prison at Bedford until 1672.

A few years before his arrest, Bunyan had moved from Elstow to St. Cuthbert's Street, Bedford, with his wife and two daughters; the youngest of whom, Mary, was born blind. Around 1659 his wife died but he soon re-married later the same year. Thus, during the course of his imprisonment at the county gaol, on the corner of High Street and Silver Street, he was able to see more of his family than might otherwise have been the case. Also, with the help of an occasional blind eye, turned by a sympathetic gaoler, he was able to slip out to preach once in a while.

Despite the inevitable hardships endured by Bunyan and his family during his intermittent twelve years' confinement, the 'Immortal Dreamer' used his time constructively, reading and studying the Bible and writing. His first tract, 'Some Gospel-Truths Opened' had been published in 1656. Written 'rapidly and in a heat', he attacked the theological soundness of the Quakers, with whom he had come into conflict. A vigorous defence of their position written by a young Quaker, Edward Burrough, caused Bunyan to rush into print again, with his reply, 'A Vindication of Gospel-Truths Opened'.

Several more tracts and books soon followed; one with the intriguing title, 'A Few Sighs from Hell' and, as Bunyan's imprisonment allowed him more time for reading and reflection, so his writing burgeoned. The principal work published during his twelve years' incarceration was a spiritual autobiography, 'Grace Abounding to the Chief of Sinners', (published in 1666), in which Bunyan related the history of his life's spiritual development, culminating in his call to the ministry.

Among Bunyan's other major works was 'The Life and Death of Mr Badman', which appeared in 1680. Allegorical and episodic in form, and didactic in tone, the book comprises a dialogue between Mr Wiseman and Mr Attentive about the godless life of the now deceased eponymous anti-hero. This was followed two years later by 'The Holy War', another allegory but written on a far larger canvas. It is possible that Bunyan had in mind his own experiences as a Parliamentary soldier garrisoned at Newport Pagnell, when he wrote and endlessly revised this convoluted tale of the city of Mansoul laid seige to by the opposing forces of good and evil. At the heart of the book, is the epic struggle between God and the Devil for the control of Man and the Universe; but the text is weighed down by spiritual debate which dissipates the story and makes it not the easiest of Bunyan's books to read.

Quite the reverse is true, however, of the one book with which John Bunyan's name has become synonymous all over the world. 'The Pilgrim's Progress', published in two parts – in 1678 and 1684 – is a model of simple and direct prose; the beauty of its language inevitably much influenced by Bunyan's long and close study of the Bible. If the book is synonymous with Bunyan, then this allegorical tale of Christian's journey from the City of Destruction to the Celestial City, is no less closely associated with Bedfordshire.

A thriving cottage industry has grown up around the endless attempts to link the various steps along the Pilgrim's journey with actual locations in the county: Cardington Brook with the 'Slough of Despond'; Houghton House with the 'House

Beautiful'; the Chilterns with the 'Delectable Mountains', and so on. But H. G. Tibbutt, in his article, 'The Pilgrim's Route', (Bedfordshire Magazine, Autumn 1959), urges a degree of caution. 'The work, after all, is a spiritual allegory,' he rightly points out. 'Any attempt to relate the topography of 'The Pilgrim's Progress' to real geography can never be more than the merest hypothesis, and there is a danger that Bunyan's great spiritual classic will be obscured by attempts to provide its incidents with factual localities.'

On the other hand, Beldfordshire was Bunyan's milieu. As the years went by he would travel further afield, into neighbouring counties and down to London for preaching engagements and sometimes – while in the capital – to supervise one of his books though the press. As a tinker, however, living first at Elstow and then in Bedford, and travelling extensively about the countryside in the course of his work, the landscape of Bedfordshire surrounded him at every turn; and it would be odd if, when he came to chart the course of Christian's journey, the familiar panorama did not impose itself on his mind's eye.

*The Bunyan Meeting, Bedford.*

'The Pilgrim's Progress', of course, is set firmly in the ranks of the world's greatest literature, and transcends any mere county boundary by its universal relevance. Nevertheless, with all its many local Bunyan associations, Bedfordshire could not fail to be the focal point for anyone with an interest in the life and work of its most famous literary son.

In addition to the Bunyan statue on St. Peter's Green in Bedford, and to the various other memorials and commemorative tablets and plaques scattered throughout the county, (and – not least – the plentiful opportunities for making connections between actual places and the steps along Christian's route), Bedfordshire houses several important Bunyan collections. The Bunyan Museum and Library at Bunyan Meeting, Mill Street, Bedford, for example, contains many English and foreign-language editions of Bunyan's works, including 'The Pilgrim's Progress' in over one hundred and sixty different editions. Many of the author's personal relics are on display, including his chair, fiddle and anvil. At Elstow, a room devoted to Bunyan's work, life and times can be found at the Moot Hall.

*The Moot Hall, Elstow.*

John Bunyan died in London, in 1688. Having travelled from Bedford to Reading, to mediate between an estranged father and son, he developed a fever after being caught in heavy rain while riding on to London to see his friend, John Strudwick, at Snow Hill. He was buried at Bunhill Fields, the 'Camp Santo of Nonconformity', as Southey called it, which also contains the graves of Daniel Defoe, Isaac Watts and William Blake. A few years earlier, and just a stone's throw away in Bunhill Row, Milton had finished 'Paradise Lost' and had written 'Paradise Regained'.

Thus Bunyan lies within earshot of the constant hum of

traffic wafting over from the City Road, and in the shadow of the Barbican's tower-blocks. It is all very far from 'Bedfordshire's homely villages and peaceful streams . . .' which, wrote Vera Brittain, 'Bunyan made . . . shine with the light of Heaven itself, and turned the life of an ordinary man struggling to overcome his daily temptations into a journey as heroic as Jason's quest for the Golden Fleece.'

# John Bunyan:

# A Progress through Hertfordshire

Although John Bunyan was essentially a Bedfordshire man and – except for the few years he served in the Parliamentary army – spent all his days either at Elstow or Bedford, he inevitably forged some links with neighbouring counties, and not least with Hertfordshire, where he sometimes undertook preaching engagements. As a result, there are some interesting reminders of him in the county although, as several of these have become well camouflaged – literally – by the passage of time, perseverance is the keyword when seeking Bunyan associations here.

Bunyan also had family connections with Hertfordshire: at Hitchin, for example where, according to the town's historian, Reginald Hine, Bunyan's Aunt Alice lived and his sister, Elizabeth, was baptized. It is thought that he had other relatives at St. Albans; a town in which he occasionally stayed and through which he passed on his way to and from London.

After his release from prison in 1672, (under the 'Declaration of Indulgence', which relaxed the laws of repression against the Independent church), Bunyan was able to apply for a licence to preach. Such religious toleration was short-lived, however, and before long he was forced once more to preach in secrecy. It was around this time that he built up a 'circuit', which took him from Bedford into Hertfordshire and Cambridgeshire, and so back to Bedfordshire again.

By dint of necessity, therefore, meetings were usually held during the hours of darkness and in sequestered spots, away from towns: barns, farmhouses and isolated cottages being much the favoured locations. It is not surprising that, in his circumstances, where the need for discretion and secrecy was paramount, Bunyan failed to keep any kind of detailed diary or documentary record; something which makes authenticated accounts of his various activities difficult to come by, and so tradition occasionally mingles with hard fact.

Rudolph Robert, quoting from the 'Victoria County History', for example, in his own book, 'Famous Authors in Hertfordshire' (1970), mentions the '. . . few old half-timber and brick cottages and a farmhouse in which it is said that John Bunyan used to preach,' at St. Paul's Walden. Welwyn Garden City also claims a connection with the 'Immortal Dreamer' who, it is believed, addressed meetings in a large barn at Handside Farm. Tangible evidence of his preaching activities at Pickerings Farm, Bendish, (a few miles from Hitchin), was later transferred to the early-twentieth century Baptist church at Breachwood Green, near King's Walden, where an oak pulpit said to have been used by Bunyan at Bendish, bearing his name and dated 1658, shows that he was already preaching in Hertfordshire before his arrest in 1660.

At the hamlet of Coleman's Green, near Wheathampstead, a lone chimney rises out of undergrowth on a piece of waste ground just off the roadside. A barely legible plaque fixed to one side of it reads: 'John Bunyan is said by tradition to have preached and occasionally to have lodged in the cottage of which this chimney was a part.' Crumbling and so long neglected, this sad ruin is in stark contrast to another, more robust reminder of Bunyan which stands on the opposite side of the road: the 'John Bunyan' pub, with its sign showing Bunyan's head and the chimney juxtaposed.

One of Bunyan's most secluded preaching stations,

however, was at Wain Wood, near Preston, just south of Hitchin where, in the natural amphitheatre of Wain Wood Dell, Bunyan would invariably attract large crowds, often running into several hundreds – and usually at night – to hear him speak. It is a spot at which pilgrims sometimes still gather from all over the world when services are held there on special occasions.

*Bunyan's Chimney, at Coleman's Green.*

In addition to John Bunyan's family connections with Hitchin a stone tablet, set into a side wall of the Baptist church in Tilehouse Street, bears witness to a rather strange link with him. The tablet commemorates Agnes Beaumont, who was buried in the Tilehouse Street churchyard after her death in 1720. 'This stone', it reads, 'was erected by Subscription in 1812, in respectful remembrance of a person so justly celebrated for her eminent piety and remarkable sufferings.'

The story of Agnes Beaumont and John Bunyan, has many of the ingredients of a Thomas Hardy novel, with its series of misunderstandings and the intervention of the untimely hand of Fate. It all began when Agnes, the pious daughter of a farmer at Edworth (near Hitchin, but over the border into Bedfordshire), and a follower of Bunyan, rode pillion on horseback with him to a church meeting in February 1674.

Agnes's father, John Beaumont, had already been turned against Bunyan by several people whose own purposes it served to denigrate the preacher. After seeing the pair together, he closed his doors against his daughter when she returned home, despite the fact that it was deep midwinter. He relented after a night or two, however, and then – quite suddenly – he died. A rumour was spread that Agnes and Bunyan had conspired to poison him, but an inquest concluded that John Beaumont had died from natural causes.

Agnes Beaumont maintained a life-long interest in the Tilehouse Street Baptist Church through her friendship with the pastor, John Wilson. Although she lived in Highgate at the time of her death, she was buried in the Hitchin graveyard at her own request.

There is, it is thought, only one contemporary portrait of John Bunyan still in existence. It was painted by Thomas Sadler a few years before the preacher's death and was discovered not in Bedfordshire, but in a cottage at Codicote, near Welwyn. The painting was purchased in 1902 by the National Portrait Gallery, where it now hangs. A copy of a detail from it may be seen gracing the head of this chapter.

*Rear view of the Baptist chapel in Tilehouse Street, Hitchin, showing a part of the graveyard.*

# Dorothy Osborne:

# Love-Letters from Chicksands

All the world, it is said, loves a lover and, if the pair in question happens to be 'star-crossed', then the fascination is all the more acute. Romeo and Juliet have become synonymous with this unfortunate condition, but the inter-family feuding and hostility which finally led to their undoing has its echoes today on a larger scale: wherever race or religion, political persuasion or any other kind of prejudice is allowed to hold sway over people's finer feelings.

In seventeenth-century England, at the time of the Civil War, Dorothy Osborne and William Temple were separated by a quarrel that was not of their making, during a period when many families were cruelly divided by their allegiance to the Roundheads or the Cavaliers. Dorothy Osborne came from a distinguished Royalist family, while the position of the Temples was slightly equivocal. William's father was a member of the Long Parliament and, more significantly his cousin, Colonel Hammond, was Commander of Carisbrooke Castle, where Charles I was imprisoned; and where also, by an odd coincidence, Dorothy's cousin, Richard, was Groom-in-waiting to the King.

A happy ending was in store for Dorothy Osborne and William Temple, although six years were to pass from their first meeting to their wedding-day. But as every cloud has a silver lining, so their story is no exception to the rule. The opposition which was raised to the match by both families allowed time for a lengthy correspondence to develop between the two lovers, and more than seventy of Dorothy's letters have been preserved. Written largely in the privacy of her home at Chicksands Priory, and for Temple's eyes alone, their main interest today rests in the vivid picture they give of daily life during a unique period in England's history.

Chicksands Priory, a few miles west of Shefford, now stands – somewhat incongruously, given its origins – within the precincts of an R.A.F. camp. During the middle of the twelfth century, the Order of Gilbert of Sempringham had founded a religious house there but, after the Dissolution, the property fell into the hands of Dorothy's great-grandfather, and Chicksands had remained in the family's possession ever since.

*Chicksands Priory today. (Open to the public: 1st & 3rd Sundays of the month, April–October, and at other times by appointment.)*

Dorothy's father, Sir Peter Osborne, had been made Governor of Guernsey in 1611; an appointment which, at first, did little to inhibit his life as a Bedfordshire country gentleman. At the outbreak of the Civil War, however, when Guernsey declared itself for Cromwell, Sir Peter took personal charge of the isolated Royalist garrison on the island. In the meantime, deeming it unwise to remain at Chicksands, as the Parliamentary faction strengthened around her in Bedfordshire, Lady Osborne sought refuge at St. Malo, where she was eventually reduced to selling her personal possessions in order to raise funds to help support her husband's starving garrison. Eventually, Sir Peter also withdrew to St. Malo, whither Dorothy – accompanied by her brother, Robin – was bound to visit him, when she called in at the Isle of Wight *en route*, to see her cousin, Richard. It was during the course of these few days in 1648 that she first met William Temple, who was staying with Colonel Hammond before setting off on his own European travels.

The couple's first meeting, however, took place in decidedly inauspicious circumstances. Robin Osborne, in a demonstration of Royalist allegiance, had scrawled a biblical quotation on a window of the inn at which he and Dorothy were staying, 'Haman,' he wrote, in a veiled though obvious reference to Hammond, 'was hanged on the gallows he had prepared for Mordecai.' Brother and sister were duly arrested, and hauled up before the Commander of Carisbrooke. Believing that the matter would be dealt with more leniently if it were found that a woman had been responsible, Dorothy confessed to the deed – and was instantly set free, with Robin! Twenty year-old William had been present throughout the interview, and fell in love with the 'stately' girl a year his senior, whose courage and initiative had saved her brother's skin.

The subsequent course of events is a little obscure, but a letter written some years later by Dorothy suggests that Temple joined the Osbornes on their journey down to St. Malo. 'Do you remember Arme [Herm], and the little house there?' she enquired of him, in one of her most charming passages. '. . . That's next to being out of the world. There we might live like Baucis and Philemon, grow old together in our little cottage, and for our charity to some ship-wrecked strangers obtain the blessing of dying both at the same time.'

But circumstances quickly conspired against the pair, as Sir William Temple ordered his son to remain abroad out of harm's way, when Dorothy returned to England with her family the following year, to pick up the threads of their old life in Bedfordshire. One can only imagine Dorothy's feelings once back at Chicksands Priory; separated from her lover, and with both parents in poor health and sadly reduced circumstances.

Dorothy clearly considered herself betrothed to William Temple although she saw nothing of him for some years, beyond the most occasional meetings in London when he temporarily returned home from his travels. In the meantime, however, she was kept busy fending off a succession of potential suitors, who were thrust in her direction by her over-zealous brother, Henry.

One of the most surprising contenders for her hand, and one who wooed her assiduously with '. . . presents of letter-seals, greyhounds and an Irish wolfhound,' was Henry Cromwell, the son of the Lord Protector. It is astonishing that the Cromwells appeared to be unconcerned about forming an alliance with such a staunchly Royalist family. By this time, there were signs that Dorothy was growing weary of resisting her family's objections to Temple. 'If I cannot be yours,' she told him, 'they may dispose of me how they please. H.C. will be as acceptable to me as anyone else.'

The letters by which Dorothy Osborne is remembered were all written within a two-year period, beginning on Christmas Eve 1652. She had not heard from Temple for over nine months, when a message arrived from him at Chicksands, informing her that he was once again back in England. 'And now, sir,' she replied, 'let me tell you that I am extremely glad to hear from you, since there are few persons in the world I am more concerned in . . .'

'Buried alive' at Chicksands, as she later described herself, there is a pervading sense in Dorothy's letters that, between nursing her by now seriously ailing father, and waiting to hear from Temple again, time hung heavily upon her. 'You ask me how I pass my time here,' she responds on one occasion. 'I can give you a perfect account not only of what I do for the present, but what I am likely to do this seven year if I stay here so long.'

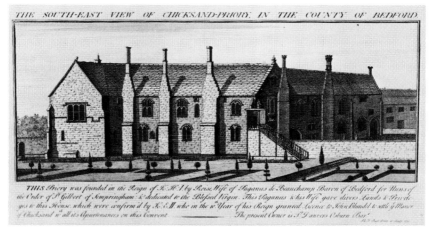

*A 1730 print of Chicksands Priory. (By kind permission
of The Friends of Chicksands Priory.)*

In another mood, she captures beautifully the pastoral quality of seventeenth-century Chicksands. '. . . About six or seven o'clock, I walk into a common that lies hard by the house where a great many wenches keep sheep and cows and sit in the shade singing of ballads; I go to them and compare their voices and beauty to some Ancient Shepherdesses that I have heard of, and find a vast difference there . . .' The sting in the tail reveals a mischievous sense of humour, which is put to good effect elsewhere. 'Let me ask you if you have seen a book of Poems newly come out, made by my Lady Newcastle. For God's sake if you meet with it send it me,' she implores William; 'they say it is ten times more extravagant than her dress.'

More often that not, however, it is Dorothy's desire to be able to share her life with William that shines through. 'I have been so persecuted with visits all this week,' she tells him, 'I have had no time to despatch anything of business, so that now I have . . . 40 letters more to write. How much rather would I have them all to you than to anyone else, or rather how much better it would be if there needed none to you and that I could tell you without writing . . .'

Deeply in love with William Temple though she was, Dorothy would not contemplate marriage to him without her father's consent and, as this was denied her, so she resisted William's constant entreaties to marry him. When Sir Peter died in the spring of 1653, however, this insurmountable barrier was removed, and despite her eldest brother's continuing displeasure the two families directly involved relented towards the couple. As a result, a wedding-date was fixed and, although at the eleventh hour Dorothy became seriously ill with smallpox, she recovered in time – although still visibly scarred – for the marriage to take place as arranged, on Christmas Day 1654.

The honeymoon was spent at Moor Park, a seventeenth-century mansion near Rickmansworth; 'the sweetest place, I think,' wrote Temple many years later, 'that I have ever seen in my life.' When he retired to Surrey after a lifetime spent in the Diplomatic Service, Temple called his house at Farnham 'Moor Park', in memory of it. There, he devoted himself to his garden and wrote essays; and he employed as his secretary a certain Jonathan Swift, who described Lady Temple as 'mild Dorothea, peaceful, wise and great.'

The marriage lasted for forty years, and was a happy one, although the Temples suffered the intense grief of losing their seven children and were, at the last, denied the blessing given to Baucis and Philemon. Dorothy died in 1695, at the age of sixty-seven, although William survived her only by four years.

# Into Exile:

# Sir Francis Bacon at Gorhambury

'So let great authors have their due,' wrote Francis Bacon, in 'The Advancement of Learning'. It is a singularly apt quotation from one who, since the middle of the nineteenth century, has been at the centre of a still-thriving debate over authorship. Did Francis Bacon write the plays attributed to William Shakespeare, or did he not? Dean Church, in his 1884 biography, asserted that '. . . Bacon could no more have written the plays than Shakespeare could have prophecied the triumphs of natural philosophy.' The argument, however, rumbles on.

What would Bacon himself have made of the controversy? If his Last Will and Testament is any indication, he would have been characteristically philosophical. 'For my name and memory,' he wrote, resignedly, 'I leave it to men's charitable speeches, and to foreign nations, and the next ages.'

Those sound like the rather weary sentiments of a man who has taken at least his fair share of life's buffets. Certainly he suffered a marked reversal of fortune during his last years when, as Lord Chancellor and at the height of his political career, he fell from grace in 1621. But, if Viscount St. Albans – as he was, by then – found himself prohibited from attending Parliament, stripped of his high office and banished, in effect, to his country seat in Hertfordshire then, on the positive side, he was able to devote the last five years of his life almost entirely to writing.

Francis Bacon was born in 1561 at York House, in the Strand. He was the younger son of Sir Nicholas Bacon, Lord Keeper of the Great Seal to Elizabeth I. Sir Nicholas had recently purchased the manor of Gorhambury, a few miles to the west of St. Albans, and had immediately set about injecting new life into the decaying estate, by building himself a country home there.

Although Sir Nicholas was undoubtedly impressed by his own handiwork, which took five years to complete, Queen Elizabeth was not over-complimentary when, in 1570, she made her first progress to Gorhambury to visit her Lord Keeper at home. 'My Lord,' she exclaimed, 'what a little house you have gotten!' 'Madam, my house is well, but it is you who have made me too great for it,' was Sir Nicholas's urbane reply. He took the implied criticism to heart, nevertheless, and added a new wing forthwith!

It was in the privileged surroundings of York House and Gorhambury, therefore, that young Francis Bacon was nurtured in the cradle of Elizabethan England. Born into a distinguished family, he enjoyed all the advantages that were attached to his father's high position in public life. The Queen herself took an early interest in Francis, calling him her 'young Lord Keeper', and maintaining a watchful eye on his progress at university.

As the exceptionally promising son of an influential father, it must have seemed inevitable to Francis Bacon that a glittering career in public life lay before him. Yet there were to be long years spent waiting in the wings, both as a lawyer and as a Member of Parliament for various constituencies, before his talents were allowed full rein.

From the time he received his knighthood in 1603, however, Bacon cut a swath through some of the highest positions in public life; from Solicitor-General in 1607 to Lord Chancellor in 1618. He was also appointed Lord Keeper of the Great Seal; an office which must have given him particular satisfaction, in view of his father's earlier connection with the post. By that time raised to the peerage as Lord Verulam, and created Viscount St. Albans in 1621 Bacon had, by the age of sixty, achieved his greatest political ambitions.

Then, literally almost overnight, his career was shattered. Charged by the House of Lords with receiving bribes and perverting the course of justice, Bacon was fined £40,000 and committed to the Tower, although both punishments were rescinded shortly afterwards. No longer Keeper of the Great Seal, however, and debarred from any further public office, Bacon left London and spent his last years almost exclusively at Gorhambury.

Francis Bacon had inherited the Hertfordshire estate during his early forties, on the death of his elder brother, Anthony. The present house, which stands close to the Roman Theatre of Verulamium, was completed in 1778, and the Tudor mansion built by Sir Nicholas lies in ruins nearby. In a fit of early enthusiasm, Francis Bacon had augmented Gorhambury by building Verulam House a mile or so away. It served as a retreat where he could write undisturbed, when Gorhambury itself was full with visitors; but it was demolished in 1663, and no trace of it remains.

*The ruins of Old Gorhambury.*

Bacon's reputation as a writer of broadly philosophical works, had been established long before his sudden disappearance from public life. The first edition of his 'Essays, or Counsels Civill and Moral', had been published in 1597, and his philosophical treatise, 'The Advancement of Learning', had appeared in 1605. This work, planned as the first part of a much larger project, called 'The Great Instauration', dealt with the 'division of the sciences', and included a survey and systematic classification of all branches of knowledge. Originally written in English, Bacon prepared a revised and expanded Latin translation, which appeared under the title, 'De Augmentis Scientiarum', in 1623.

The second instalment of this massive undertaking, the 'Novum Organum', (literally, the 'New Instrument'), was published in Latin, in 1620, the year before Bacon's premature retirement. Bacon was deeply interested in the possibilities of scientific experimentation as a means of increasing Man's knowledge and control of the natural world around him. In the 'Novum Organum', he outlined his own ideas on new – and, he believed – more reliable means of scientific enquiry.

Bacon conceived of 'The Great Instauration' in five parts, but he died before the task was completed. A third – although unfinished – book in the cycle, 'Sylva Sylvarum', dealing with natural phenomena was published posthumously, in 1627, but the rest remained unwritten.

A third edition of Bacon's 'Counsels, Civill and Moral', appeared in 1625, by which time the original collection of ten essays – and a second enlarged edition – had been expanded to fifty-eight. Their range is broad and diverse, extending from a discourse on gardens to reflections on such abstract topics as 'Truth' and 'Unity'. Overflowing with aphorisms, they offer – in a style characterized by short, pithy sentences – 'wise counsel for the successful conduct of life and the management of men.'

Other fruits of Bacon's retirement included 'The New Atlantis', which was also published posthumously in 1627. Following a hundred years or so after Thomas More had coined the word, Bacon's fable – partly philosophical, partly political – describes life among a Utopian community on an imaginary Pacific island. Bacon also published an important biography of Henry VII, in 1622, from which, according to James Spedding, who edited a seven-volume edition of Bacon's works during the 1850s, 'every history which has been written since has derived all its light . . . and followed its guidance in every question of importance.'

Although he was debarred from entering into the life of Parliament, it is obvious from the sheer bulk of his output that Bacon was anything but short of employment at Gorhambury. He had longed for leisure during the hectic years of political life in London and, when it came – albeit unexpectedly – he used it well. It was fortunate that country life suited him, and that he was able to divide his time between the house his father had built, and his own creation, Verulam House.

At one stage Gorhambury House, well in advance of its time, had running water in every room, piped from ponds in nearby Pre (or Prae) Wood. By the time that Francis Bacon inherited the property, however, the water had ceased. This was one of the considerations which had influenced the position of Verulam House. 'Since he could not carry the water to his house,' explained Bacon's chaplain, Dr Rawley, 'he would carry his house to the water.'

Although Bacon was in his mid-sixties his death, when it came, was quite unexpected, and it occurred just at the time when – although further high office was out of the question – his star was rising once again in the firmament of the Court and Parliament. The events leading up to his death have been well-rehearsed: how on a cold day in March 1626, *en route* from London to Gorhambury, he halted in a snowstorm, and bought a chicken already prepared for the pot. Filling the cavity with snow, he settled back to observe the preserving effects of primitive refrigeration. Unfortunately he caught a chill in the process, which soon turned to bronchial pneumonia and, within a few days, he was dead. Thus ended a life and a career which, according to Dean Church, 'with all its glories . . . was the greatest shipwreck, the greatest tragedy of an age which saw many.'

Francis Bacon left instructions that he should be laid to rest in St. Michael's church, St. Albans. 'It is the parish church of my mansion house of Gorhambury,' he noted in his Will, 'and the only Christian church within the walls of ancient Verulam.' But his actual resting-place is unknown, and remains a mystery as deep as that surrounding the identity of

*St. Michael's, Gorhambury.*

the sculptor of the distinctive Bacon statue on the north side of the chancel in St. Michael's. Some people, including the diarist,

*The Bacon Statue, in St. Michael's.*

John Evelyn, have found the monument – which shows Bacon casually seated and wearing a wide-brimmed hat – too irreverent for their tastes. It was erected by Bacon's friend and secretary, Thomas Meautys, and bears three Latin inscriptions; the second of which might have particularly appealed to the late Viscount St. Albans,

> 'Who after all Natural Wisdom
> And secrets of Civil Life he
> had unfolded,
> Nature's Law fulfilled –
> Let Compounds be dissolved!
> in the year of Our Lord
> 1626, aged 66.

# George Chapman:

## 'The Learned Shepherd' of Hitchin

George Chapman, the Elizabethan poet, playwright and translator, is now probably the least remembered of an intimate circle which included Edmund Spenser, Ben Johnson and Christopher Marlowe, and which was presided over by William Shakespeare. His name will be familiar to the general reader today, however, because of Keats's sonnet, 'On First Looking into Chapman's Homer', which begins with the famous line: 'Much have I travelled in the realms of gold . . .' and was composed two centuries after Chapman's translations of 'The Iliad' and 'The Odyssey' first appeared. They were the crowning achievements of his life, and a labour of love which occupied him for twenty-six years.

Inevitably, when considering the life of someone who was born over four hundred years ago, 'wild surmise' must often take the place of concrete evidence. Parish records, where they exist at this time, are often found to be lacking, so that speculation based upon what fragments of documentary proof are available has to be the order of the day.

It is thought that George Chapman was born at Hitchin, and almost certainly in 1559. There are no parish records to confirm this, however, as they do not begin until three years later, and the issue was further clouded by Chapman's first biographer. Anthony à Wood, who suggested that Chapman's family came from Kent. The weight of evidence, however, not least from Chapman's own pen, swings heavily in Hitchin's favour. In his poem, 'Euthymiae Raptus, or The Teares of Peace', published in 1609, he describes how once, in a dream, the ghost of Homer had appeared to him on Hitchin Hill:

'I am (said he) that Spirit Elysian
That (in thy native air and on the hill
Next Hitchin's left hand) did thy bosom fill
With such a flood of soul . . .'

William Browne, writing four years later in his 'Britannia's Pastorals', described George Chapman as 'the learned shepherd of faire Hitchinge Hill'.

If this were not sufficient to convince us of George Chapman's close connection with the town then the findings of Reginald Hine, published in his book, 'Hitchin Worthies' in 1932 – an indispensable source for any student of Chapman's Hertfordshire associations – should remove any reasonable doubt on the subject. While searching in the files at Somerset House, Hine discovered the Will, dated 1581, of Chapman's father, 'Thomas Chapman of Hutchin, in the countie of Hertford, yeoman.' Among the many directions included are that he '. . . shall be decently interred within the churchyarde of Hutchin . . . uppon the place wheare Joane my late wife was buried . . .' There then follows a gift to '. . . the pore people of Hutchin . . .' and bequests for his two sons, George and Thomas. The elder of the brothers, Thomas, was to have '. . . the messuage [dwelling-house] or tenement whearin I now inhabit and dwell . . .' George was to receive £100 and two silver spoons.

A great deal of importance has been placed – by those researchers over the years seeking to identify the exact location of Chapman's birth – on the line in 'Teares of Peace', which says that he was '. . . on the hill next Hitchin's left hand,' Western House, much rebuilt since Elizabethan times, and known in more recent years as 35 Tilehouse Street, would seem to be the most likely candidate. A memorial plaque on the wall states that Chapman lived there, but it leaves unanswered the question whether or not he was actually born there.

*George Chapman's former home in Tilehouse Street, Hitchin.*

The Chapmans, in fact, had already been associated with Hertfordshire for a considerable time before George Chapman appeared on the scene. The manor of Mardocks, a small estate situated on the River Ash between Wareside and Isneye, in the parish of Stanstead Abbots, had apparently been held by the family from 1420 to 1580 and in George Chapman's day, although by no means wealthy they were, nevertheless, a family of some local standing. That same Thomas Chapman who was George's father was, at one period, holder of '. . . the Bailliwick of Hutchin under Exchequer seal.' At the end of the nineteenth century a branch of the family then still living in the town, included Fred Chapman, of the famous publishing firm, Chapman and Hall, whose authors included Dickens, Trollope and Mrs Gaskell.

At the time of George Chapman's birth, Hitchin was no more than a tiny hamlet situated – then, as now – on the River Hiz. Hardly anything at all is known about Chapman's childhood, but there is nothing to suggest that he did not follow what would have been the usual course for a lad in his position. On the opposite side of Tilehouse Street from Western House was an old school, and Chapman probably received his basic education there, before going on to a university at about the age of fifteen. It is not clear which of the two universities – Oxford or Cambridge – he attended, and there is even a suggestion that he went to both. The only certainty is that he failed to take a degree.

A similar haze obscures Chapman's next movements. Reports that he immediately established himself in London, prior to setting off for the Netherlands as a soldier, conflict somewhat with Hitchin tradition, which insists that he spent some time at his birthplace as a schoolmaster; a view which is shared by Reginald Hine, Hitchin's and the twentieth-century's own local authority on the subject. Hine believes that it was not until 1590/1, when Chapman was in his early thirties and had just come into his legacy, that he left teaching behind and moved to London to make a name for himself. Perhaps this was so, as it was not until 1594 that George Chapman's first group of poems, 'The Shadow of Night', was published. In the absence of making his living by writing, a teaching career – during the fourteen or so years since his undergraduate days – would seem feasible.

Once he was established in London, however, Chapman produced poems and plays at a furious rate, but he was both fortunate and unfortunate to be a part of the Elizabethan literary scene. On the one hand he was stimulated but, on the other, ultimately overshadowed by the circle in which he moved, containing as it did an unparalleled flowering of poets and dramatists. In his own day, however, Chapman's reputation was high among his peers. No less a genius than Shakespeare described him as '. . . a spirit by spirits taught to write above a mortal.'

In the great melting-pot of talent that was Elizabethan literary London, when the demand for new plays was immense and pressing deadlines were a constant headache, it was not unknown for one writer to begin a play and for another to complete it, in an attempt to speed up the process. One such collaboration, involving Chapman, Ben Jonson and John Marston, in 1605, on a comedy called 'Eastward Hoe', led to a short spell of imprisonment for its three authors. Elizabeth I had died in 1603, and James I (James VI of Scotland), had succeeded her. He took exception, by all accounts, to the anti-Scottish satire in the play, and threatened the culprits with slit ears and noses. However, after much wheedling by the three parties concerned, they were released unharmed.

Chapman's own comedies and tragedies are not generally well-known today. 'The Blind Beggar of Alexandria', 'May-Day', 'The Gentleman Usher' and 'Bussy D'Ambois' are a mere handful of the many plays he wrote, and he was also a prolific poet; yet he is probably as rarely performed as quoted. He recognized, however, that the great work of his life was his translation – from the Greek into English – of Homer. When, after twenty-six years, the task was finally completed, (dwarfing the mere ten years Dr Johnson spent in compiling his Dictionary), Chapman declared, with an obvious sense of relief, that '. . . the work I was born to do is done.'

'Rich enough in coined words,' as Reginald Hine expressed it, (in fact, dictionary-makers are agreed that Chapman contributed more words to the English language than any other Elizabethan writer, including Shakespeare), '. . . he was poor in coin of the realm.' He found the utmost difficulty in obtaining a steady patron and he appears to have been, more often than not, in financial straits. It seems that not even his elder brother, at home in Hitchin, could be of any assistance. Although, in the meantime, Thomas had raised himself in status from 'yeoman' (like his father before him), to 'Gent.', financial reverses had forced him to sell the Hertfordshire house in 1597.

George Chapman died – almost certainly in poverty – in London, on 12th May 1634, and was buried in the churchyard of St. Giles-in-the-Fields. A monument to him, erected over his grave by a close friend, Inigo Jones, was later moved inside the church. Although Chapman was in good company – Andrew Marvell and James Shirley were buried at St. Giles's, too – the parish which, in their day, was a rural spot, is now a throbbing artery between Charing Cross Road and Shaftesbury Avenue. It is a far cry indeed from sixteenth-century Hertfordshire, where Chapman had spent his childhood and where – if only in a dream – the ghost of Homer had appeared to him on Hitchin Hill.

# George Gascoigne:

# The 'Common Rymer' of Cardington

The name of George Gascoigne does not immediately spring to mind, in the long and distinguished catalogue of Elizabethan courtier-adventurer-poets; and yet he was a formative influence in his day. 'Gascoigne,' it was written, in 1615, 'first brake the ice for our quainter poets that now write, that they might the more safer swimme in the maine ocean of sweet poesy.' Forty years earlier though, shortly before his death, he had been disparagingly referred to in an anonymous letter sent to the Privy Council, as a 'common Rymer'.

For one whose life was so varied and short – he died in 1577, in early middle-age – Gascoigne was nevertheless a literary pioneer of some signficance. According to C. T. Prouty, whose scholarly biography of the poet appeared in 1942, Gascoigne was the first person to write an English treatise on poetry and his series of love-poems, 'Dan Bartholomew of Bathe', published in his collection, 'A Hundreth Sundrie Flowres', anticipated the Elizabethan vogue for sonnets. His masques, written in 1575, to celebrate Elizabeth I's progress at

Kenilworth and, later that year, at Woodstock, were among the earliest English dramatic entertainments of their kind and 'The Supposes', his version of Ariosto's 'I Suppositi', was the first prose comedy to be translated from the Italian.

The list of literary innovation is seemingly endless. 'The Spoyle of Antwerpe', his eye-witness account of the sacking of that city in 1576, is one of the earliest known examples of 'on-the-spot' news-reporting, while his novella, 'The Adventures of F. J.' is, according to Prouty, '. . . the first purely English story of the Renaissance, and its equal is not found until the eighteenth century.' In literature, therefore, as in his life Gascoigne – courtier, soldier, politician, farmer and all-round man of letters – was nothing if not versatile. But, even so, his reputation has entirely failed to keep pace with the likes of Spenser, Ralegh, Sidney and many other of his contemporaries.

The roots of the Gascoigne family had not dug very deep into Bedfordshire soil when George, the eldest son of Sir John Gascoigne, was born – probably at Cardington Manor – about the year 1534–5. The family had moved south from Yorkshire only a few generations earlier. It was George's grandfather, Sir William Gascoigne, who had established the family at the Tudor house which stood on a moated site, a mile or so from Cardington on the road to Old Warden.

The passage of time has obscured much of the fine detail of George Gascoigne's life. Presumably, a great deal of his childhood was spent on the family's Bedfordshire estate before he went up to Trinity College, Cambridge and then – in 1555 – to Gray's Inn, to study law. Prouty refers to the account of an incident which occurred in Cardington Wood during 1557, and which provides a glimpse of George Gascoigne at home. He made one of a party, led by his father, engaged in hot pursuit of a neighbour, Edmund Conquest, who had trespassed on Sir John's property while out hunting a stag. Sir John, when he caught up with the offender, struck '. . . with a long staff at Conquest's arms, so that the latter lost the use of both his arms and hands . . . Sir John, not therewithal contented, eftsoons struck at him again so furiously and unmanfully, that his own company bade him cease for shame.'

Hot-blooded, quarrelsome and of a litigious turn of mind: these were among the unwelcome attributes that Sir John passed down to his eldest son, and it was an inheritance that George Gascoigne would have done better without. His adult life was punctuated by legal disputes, with his own family and neighbours alike, reducing him – at one stage – to virtual bankruptcy.

*Cardington Manor House. (Photo: from the Local Studies Collection, Bedford Central Library.)*

Gascoigne spent almost a decade at Gray's Inn, during which time he entered Parliament as Burgess for Bedford Borough, perhaps through the influence of his father, who was M. P. for Bedford County. Both father and son were in the Commons to hear Elizabeth proclaimed Queen of England, following Mary's death.

Elizabeth, more than any other Tudor monarch, perhaps, drew fashionable young men to Court rather like moths around a flame, and Gascoigne could not resist the possibility of coming to her notice. The Court was all-powerful, and it had much in the way of preferment to bestow; with luck it could be a rapid path to fame and fortune and much less of a grind than the law! Gascoigne left Gray's Inn but, unfortunately, the gamble did not pay off. He failed to achieve any royal recognition and – his lavish expenditure far outstripping his income – he was forced to return to Bedfordshire to lick his wounds, and to live quietly in retirement.

By now, Gascoigne had married Elizabeth Bacon, a twice-wed and reasonably wealthy widow with whom, in 1563, he leased the manor of Willington, near Cardington, from John Gostwick. London drew him like a magnet, however, and within a few years he was back at Gray's Inn and dabbling once again at Court. Still unable to maintain the considerable expense that such a life-style required, a lack of funds drove him back to Bedfordshire once more; this time to farm on the family estate at Cardington.

*Willington Dovecote, built by Cardinal Wolsey's Master of the Horse, and now in the hands of the National Trust.*

Gascoigne's financial troubles were exacerbated during these years by the various law-suits in which he became embroiled. He was in dispute with his brother over the ownership of the manor of Fenlake Barnes, the parsonage on the Cardington estate, and he was at odds with John Gostwick about the lease at Willington. Furthermore, he was constantly beset by internecine wrangling over his inheritance and the various claims of his wife's children by her previous marriages, and he was in dispute with the Earl of Bedford, possibly concerning the ownership of some land. The result was that, at his lowest ebb, during the spring of 1570, Gascoigne was committed to Bedford Gaol for debt.

At that point, Gascoigne's trail understandably goes cold for a while but, two years later, we find him setting out as a soldier of fortune to the Low Countries. If it was his intention to recover his losses then he failed dismally, and he returned to England in the same forlorn condition that he had left it; but he did come back with a fresh determination to succeed. Having been brought to his knees, he felt that it was time to put his life into some kind of proper order and poetry, he thought, might be the answer to all his troubles.

George Gascoigne had dabbled in literature for many years; his translation of 'Jocasta', after all, had been staged in 1566, and his poems had always enjoyed a fair degree of popularity at Court and among his friends. He determined to find a patron and succeeded with Arthur, Lord Grey of Wilton, who had estates in Bedfordshire. Gascoigne's collection, 'A Hundreth Sundrie Flowres' duly appeared in 1573, while the poet himself was abroad again in Holland, either soldiering or evading creditors, or both! When he returned to England the following year, it was to be greeted by a storm of disapproval over the '. . . sundrie wanton speeches and lascivious phrases' that were to be found in his book. Nothing daunted, however, he revised the offending material and re-issued the work under a new title: 'The Poesies of George Gascoigne'.

With that, the tide had turned to some extent. A commission from the Earl of Leicester, in 1575, to write an entertainment to be given during the Queen's visit to Kenilworth – and, a few months later, to Woodstock – did much to satisfy Gascoigne's desire for royal favour. Royal patronage, when it came, arrived in the form of a request, during the summer of 1576, for him to visit the Low Countries, not as a soldier on this occasion but as a government observer. Out of this visit came 'The Spoyle of Antwerpe'.

Much of George Gascoigne's later work was of a piece with one who had seen the two days of wealth and poverty, success and failure; and of somebody who had pierced the illusion of fashionable, spendthrift living. The popular love-poetry of his first collection was supplanted by more didactic pieces. 'A delicate Diet, for daintie-mouthde Droonkardes', published in 1576, is one of the earliest dissertations on temperance in the language and 'The Grief of Joye', which appeared during the same year, is a sober reflection on mortality: on the ephemeral nature of youth and beauty, and the irrelevance of ambition in the face of that great leveller, Death. 'The ydle poett, wryting tryfles,' it was said, became 'Gascoigne the Satyricall wryter, medytating eche Muse that [might] expresse his reformacon.'

George Gascoigne died in October 1577, while on a visit to his friend, the poet George Whetstone, near Stamford. His death occurred only four years after the publication of 'A Hundreth Sundrie Flowres', and at a time when his growing reputation had been confirmed by the recent interest the Queen had taken in his work.

Before long, Gascoigne's family itself had entirely died out in Bedfordshire and now – over four hundred years later – there is little to suggest that he once had such a close connection with the county. There is no gravestone – he was buried in the Whetstone's family vault in Lincolnshire – and not even Cardington Manor remains. Its Tudor origins were subsequently overlaid with Georgian, Edwardian and Victorian alterations, until the house was finally demolished some years ago. Arthur Ransome described it, in 'The Bedfordshire Times', at the beginning of this century, as 'an interesting remnant . . .'; a phrase, perhaps, which might not unfairly be applied to one of its former occupants: George Gascoigne, the 'common Rymer' of Cardington.

# Keeping Faith:

# Sir Thomas More at Potters Bar

'Fare well my deare childe and praye for me, and I shall for you and all your freindes that we maie merily meete in heaven.' Thus ends Sir Thomas More's last letter to his daughter, Margaret Roper, written on the evening of 5th July 1535 and displaying all the self-command and enduring faith that were characteristic of him. The following morning he went calmly to the scaffold, asking the Lieutenant of the Tower to '. . . see me safe up, and my coming down let me shift for myself.'

Sir Thomas More must surely be one of the most famous Lord Chancellors in the history of that office. The story of his rise to a position of near-boon companionship with Henry VIII, and the reasons for his subsequent fall from royal favour are well-known; not least, in recent years, through the film of Robert Bolt's play, 'A Man for All Seasons'. To a whole cinema-going generation, More's quiet dignity and gentle humour and, above all, his humility, were personified by Paul Scofield's memorable portrayal of the man on the screen.

Sir Thomas More was the victim of an unfortunate twist of

Fate. Put more simply, he was in the wrong place at the wrong time. Following hard upon the annulment of his marriage to Catherine of Aragon, Henry VIII had married Anne Boleyn in 1533; a train of events which resulted in an irrevocable breach with Rome. The King renounced Papal authority and declared himself Head of the Church of England.

Sir Thomas More was just one of many who were required – by Henry – to swear to the Act of Succession; the preamble to which denied the power of the Pope. As a devout Catholic, More found himself in an impossible position and quite unable to swear to an Act which, he believed, violated the law of God and Magna Carta. In 1535, after resisting all further attempts at persuasion, More was confined to the Tower; shortly after which he was tried and found guilty of high treason, and subsequently executed.

On the face of it, these great affairs of State, played out on the international stage, would seem to be little to our purpose. But Sir Thomas More had a close link with Hertfordshire, and tradition states that much of his most famous book, 'Utopia', was actually written at his country seat, situated just north of Potters Bar.

Sir Thomas More was born in London, in 1478, the son of a judge, Sir John More. After attending St. Anthony's School in Threadneedle Street he spent some time, as was usual then, in a nobleman's household – in his case, that of Cardinal Morton, Archbishop of Canterbury – before going on to university, at Oxford. Afterwards, he studied law at Lincoln's Inn and was called to the Bar; soon distinguishing himself in his father's profession.

More entered Parliament in 1504, when he was still only in his late twenties. At the age of fifty-one, after a distinguished political career which had included his appointment as a Privy Councillor, in 1518, and which had gained him the friendship and confidence of Henry VIII, he became the first layman to fill the post of Lord Chancellor. He replaced Cardinal Wolsey who had – rather ominously, in the circumstances, and anticipating More's own fate – lost Henry's favour.

The More family's connection with Hertfordshire is said to date back at least to the fourteenth century. Rudolph Robert, writing in his comprehensive book, 'Famous Authors in

Hertfordshire' (1970), quotes from the findings of a seventeenth-century local historian, Nathaniel Salmon, on the subject. The Manor of More Hall – also known as Gobions or Gubbins – he states, '. . . was held by Sir Richard Gobion in the reign of Stephen, but the first authenticated mention of it is in 1300, when Roger de Bakesworth, on granting his share of the manor of North Mymms to his brother, Richard, retired to a certain manor of the Hospitallers called More Hall, where he died . . In 1500 it was held by Sir John More, father of Thomas More, Lord Chancellor, who is said to have written 'Utopia' there.'

Maberley Phillips, writing in a 1902 edition of the 'Home Counties Magazine' states quite confidently that, in 1390, '. . . the ancient manor of More Hall, otherwise Gobions or Gubbins,' (and later embraced by the nearby manor of Brookmans), was owned by 'John More, mercer, citizen of London.'

Whether or not the world-famous 'Utopia' was actually written at Gobions must, in the final analysis – through sheer lack of hard evidence one way or the other – remain a moot point; although, as Rudolph Robert says, 'tradition is often proved right.' At the very least, however, he must have developed many of the ideas it contained while ambling in the pleasant glades which comprised much of the Mores' small estate.

'Utopia' was published – in Latin – in 1516, and the printing of the original edition was supervised in Louvain by the Dutch scholar, Erasmus, with whom More had first come into contact while studying law at Lincoln's Inn. The work soon became popular, although it was not translated into English until 1551; when it appeared in several other European languages around the same time.

The word 'Utopia', which was coined by More and means, literally, 'no place', has passed into the language to describe virtually any type of ideal state; in that sense, it has become all things to all men. More, however, wrote about a specific idyll. His Utopia was to be found on a Pacific island, where the inhabitants had discovered the key to prosperity and happiness through a perfect – and democratic – system of government. Written over five hundred years ago, in a Tudor

England where the tyranny of the Monarch and an absence of personal freedom were exemplified by More's own death (although personal freedom was not one of Utopia's strong points, it must be said), More was far ahead of his time in espousing – in his model society – concepts which are enshrined in the welfare state of the twentieth century.

'Utopia' was far from being Sir Thomas More's only literary work – his 'History of Richard III' appeared posthumously in 1543 and he wrote extensively on theological matters, devoting much time during the last few months of his life to the task – but it was, and still is, the most significant. His book gave its name to a literary genre which includes Bacon's 'New Atlantis', William Morris's 'News from Nowhere' and Swift's 'Gulliver's Travels'. During the twentieth century, Huxley's 'Brave New World' and Orwell's 'Nineteen Eighty-Four' have been termed 'dystopian', in their depiction of societies which are the antithesis of More's ideal vision.

When More resigned as Lord Chancellor in 1532, after only three years in office, the nature of his differences with Henry persuaded him to keep a low profile. He lived quietly at Chelsea

*The 'Folly Gates' at Little Heath, Potters Bar.*

and also, one can suppose, at Gobions, during the period that he was steadfastly resisting all entreaties to swear to the Act of Succession.

In the event, More's conscience was to cost him not only his life; it also deprived his eldest son, John, of his inheritance. After his death, More's estate was confiscated by the King, although it was to briefly pass back into the hands of the family later, during the reign of Queen Mary I.

In 1836, William Gaussen purchased Gobions, at which time the estate was absorbed into the manor of Brookmans. It was Gaussen, in fact, who demolished More's house, so that, by 1935, when More was canonized four hundred years after his death, the only tangible reminder of his residence in Hertfordshire was the brick-built arched entrance to his old estate. Fondly known as the 'Folly Gates', there is some dispute about their origin; although one theory asserts that they were built during More's time, to commemorate a visit made by Henry VIII to his Lord Chancellor's Hertfordshire manor, during the sunnier days of 1530.

# Loose Ends (3)

## Nicholas Rowe

Nicholas Rowe provides ample evidence that the office of Poet Laureate is no guarantee of lasting fame. Barely remembered today, his plays and poems nevertheless earned him a coveted place in Poets' Corner, at Westminster Abbey, when he died in December 1718.

Rowe was born at Little Barford, on the very edge of Bedfordshire, in June 1674. He spent the first four years of his life in the village but, when his mother died, he moved to London with his father, who was a lawyer. Nicholas also entered the legal profession and was called to the Bar in 1694. By that time, however, his father was dead; leaving him £300 a year and the means to pursue his interest in literature.

Rowe's first tragedy, 'The Ambitious Stepmother', was produced in 1700, to great acclaim. Other successes followed and he was appointed Poet Laureate in 1715. Forgotten though his own plays may be, his six-volume edition of Shakespeare's works was a landmark in English literary history, supplying stage directions in the text and defining acts and scenes for the first time.

Pope, who wrote Rowe's epitaph, described him as 'the best of men', and Dr Johnson said that '. . . he always delights the ear and often improves the understanding.'

## Elkanah Settle

The dramatist, Elkanah Settle, had a longer but distinctly more chequered career than his Bedfordshire contemporary,

Nicholas Rowe. Born at Dunstable in February 1648, probably in the Nag's Head Tavern, which was owned by his father, Settle was still only eighteen and a student at Oxford, when his first – and very successful – play, 'Cambyses', was produced in London. He left university, however, without taking his degree, but with the prospect of a glittering career ahead of him.

To some extent, this promise was fulfilled. A few years later Settle's next play, 'The Empress of Morocco', was presented before the King at Whitehall but, during the 1680s, the man who had been considered a rival even to Dryden, lost public favour as a dramatist and drifted into political journalism. Not even his later appointment as the City Poet, requiring him to write pageants for the Lord Mayor's Show, nor further successes in the theatre – innovatory productions in which he combined dialogue and operatic interludes, thus paving the way for the likes of John Gay – could prevent Elkanah Settle from dying in poverty, in 1724.

# John Donne

John Donne, widely regarded as the founder and leading exponent of the Metaphysical 'school' of poetry, was the rector of Blunham for almost a decade, until his death in 1631. But the inhabitants of this predominantly market-gardening community saw little – if anything – of their distinguished incumbent. Local tradition asserts that he once returned to London accompanied by a cart-load of cucumbers, so he must have visited the parish at least occasionally. There is scant evidence, however, to suggest that he actually preached in the village church of St. Edmund; and a silver communion chalice and paten, which he presented to the church in 1626, is probably the most tangible reminder of his connection with the place.

Born of Roman Catholic parents, in 1572, Donne later renounced Catholicism and, after a chequered and precarious career in public service, took Anglican Holy Orders in 1615; by which time much of his poetry had been written although, with the exception of two funeral elegies, none of it appeared until 1633, two years after his death. In 1621, he was installed as

Dean of St. Paul's; a factor which may have contributed to his absence from Blunham.

# Sir Horace Walpole

Sir Horace Walpole was the author of the famous 'Gothic' novel, 'The Castle of Otranto', which appeared in 1764. But his literary reputation rests mainly upon his often very witty letters which, written to a wide circle of correspondents over a period of sixty years, show that he was no stranger to Bedfordshire.

Two particular friends, with whom Walpole corresponded at length, were the Earl and Countess of Upper Ossary, whose home at Ampthill Park was always open to him. 'I dote on Ampthill,' he wrote to the Countess on one occasion, and he often made the journey from his own home at Strawberry Hill, Twickenham, to stay there or at nearby Houghton House where the Ossarys also lived for a short time. In an uncharacteristically acerbic mood, Walpole described Houghton as the 'worst contrived' house he had ever seen.

At Ampthill, Walpole was instrumental in erecting the Katherine Cross, on the site of the former Ampthill Castle, where Katherine of Aragon had once been detained. Shortly before his death in 1797, at the age of eighty, he likened himself to the Cross, which had recently been damaged in a storm: '. . . only enough remains to preserve my name a little longer,' he wrote, 'and then the grass will cover us both.'

# Thomas Norton

Thomas Norton was not only a playwright but also, to some who knew him, 'The Rack-master General of Sharpenhoe'. Posterity, it must be said, remembers him for the latter rather than the former role, despite the fact that, as co-author – with Thomas Sackville – of the first English tragedy to be written in blank verse, (called 'The Tragedy of Ferrex and Porrex', later known as 'Gorboduc'), he holds a unique place in the history of English literature.

Thomas Norton was born in 1532, probably in London, although he had a close link with Bedfordshire as his father owned Sharpenhoe Manor, in the parish of Streatley. A poet, playwright and translator, Norton was also a lawyer and a Member of Parliament. The sobriquet which was applied to him, however, had its origins in darker deeds. He was ardently anti-Catholic, and given to using the rack when persecuting members of the faith.

Although work caused him to spend much of his time in London, Norton was a frequent visitor to the Bedfordshire estate which had passed into his hands after his father's death. Barely a year later, however, in March 1584, Norton himself died there, and was buried at Streatley church, nearby.

# Acknowledgements

The author would like to thank the following for granting permission to quote from copyright material:

For extracts from Graham Greene's 'A Sort of Life', 'The Human Factor', and 'The Lost Childhood' (from Collected Essays), The Executors of Graham Greene and The Bodley Head Ltd.; for an extract from 'The Innocent' (from Collected Stories), the Executors of Graham Greene, The Bodley Head Ltd. and William Heinemann Ltd,; for an extract from George Orwell's Diaries, the Estate of the late Sonia Brownell Orwell and Martin Secker & Warburg Ltd.; for extracts from 'Sir Albert Richardson: The Professor', Simon Houfe and White Crescent Press Ltd,; for extracts from 'E. M. Forster: A Life', P. N. Furbank and Martin Secker & Warburg Ltd.; for extracts from the 'Rooksnest' Appendix to E. M. Forster's 'Howards End' and extracts from the short-story, 'Ansell', Edward Arnold (Publishers); for extracts from 'The Letters of Arnold Bennett' Vol. 2, Edited by James Hepburn (OUP), and from 'The Journals of Arnold Bennett' Vol. 1, edited by Sir Newman Flower (Cassell & Co. Ltd.), A. P. Watt Ltd., on behalf of Madame V. Eldin; for extracts from 'The Journal of Beatrix Potter: 1881–1897', transcribed by Leslie Linder, Margaret Lane's 'The Tale of Beatrix Potter' and Beatrix Potter's 'Cecily Parsley's Nursery Rhymes', Frederick Warne; for extracts from Andrew Birkin's 'J. M. Barrie and the Lost Boys', Constable & Co. Ltd.; for extracts from Allan Chappelow's 'Shaw the Chucker-Out', Unwin Hyman Ltd., (part of HarperCollins Publishers); for lines from Bernard Shaw's 'Rhyming Picture Guide to Ayot St. Lawrence' (Leagrave Press Ltd.), the Society of Authors on behalf of the Bernard Shaw Estate; for extracts from J. P. Trevelyan's 'The Life of Mrs Humphry Ward', Constable & Co. Ltd., and for extracts from Enid Huws Jones's 'Mrs Humphry Ward', William Heinemann Ltd.

Acknowledgement is also made to Elizaveta Fen, for the quotation from 'George Orwell's First Wife: A Memoir', published in 'Twentieth Century', August 1960, and to Allan Chappelow for extracts from 'Shaw the Villager and Human-Being', (Charles Skilton Ltd.). For extracts from 'The Letters of Charles and Mary Lamb', Edited by E. W. Marrs, the Cornell University Press; for an extract from James King's 'William Cowper. A Biography', the Duke University Press, and for an extract from 'The Letters and Prose Writings of William Cowper', Vol. 1 (1750–1781), Edited by J. King & C. Ryskamp, Oxford University Press.

All photographs in the main body of the text were taken by the author, unless otherwise stated. All vignettes were supplied by, and are the copyright of, the National Portrait Gallery, except for the following: George Orwell, (Orwell Archive, University College London); George Gascoigne, (British Museum); Mark Rutherford, (Mayor and Corporation of Bedford); Worthington George Smith, (White Crescent Press Ltd.); Sir Albert Richardson, (Simon Houfe); George Chapman, (original source unknown).

# Bibliography

In addition to the specific sources mentioned below, any book about the literary associations of Hertfordshire and Bedfordshire can only be enhanced by the rich treasury of articles on the subject, which have appeared over many years in the pages of 'Hertfordshire Countryside', (where a number of the chapters in this present volume first saw the light of day in another form), and in the pages of 'Bedfordshire Magazine'. While it would be impossible to list such a large army of contributors individually, their work forms an invaluable background to any serious study in this field.

Bennett, Arnold, Teresa of Watling Street,
  The Book Castle, Dunstable, 1989.
Bennett, Arnold, The Journals, Vol. 1,
  Edited by Sir Newman Flower, Cassell & Co. Ltd., 1932.
Bennett, Arnold, The Letters, Vol. 2,
  Edited by James Hepburn, OUP, 1968.
Birkin, Andrew, J. M. Barrie and the Lost Boys,
  Constable & Co. Ltd., 1979.
Blyth, Henry, Caro: The Fatal Passion,
  History Book Club, 1972.
Brittain, Vera, In the Steps of John Bunyan,
  Rich & Cowan, 1950.
Chappelow, Allan, Shaw the Villager and Human-Being,
  Charles Skilton Ltd., 1961.
Cowper, William, The Letters, Edited by E. V. Lucas,
  OUP, 1908.
Crick, Bernard, George Orwell: A Life,
  Martin Secker & Warburg Ltd., 1980.
Dexter, W, Dickens in Hertfordshire,
  Undated Pamphlet.

Dunbar, Janet, J. M. Barrie: The Man Behind the Image, Collins, 1970.

Dyer, James, Worthington George Smith, B.H.R.S., Vol. 57, 1978.

Ellis, Peter Berresford, & Williams, Piers, 'By Jove, Biggles!': The Life of Captain W. E. Johns, W. H. Allen, 1981.

Evans, Vivienne, John Bunyan: His Life and Times, The Book Castle, Dunstable, 1988.

Flower, Sibylla Jane, Bulwer-Lytton, Shire, 1973.

Forster, Harold, Edward Young: Poet of the Night Thoughts, 1683–1765, Erskine, Aldeburgh, 1986.

Fry, Christopher, Can You Find Me – A Family History, OUP, 1978.

Furbank, P.N., E. M. Forster: A Life, 2 Vols., Martin Secker & Warburg Ltd., 1977/78.

Greene, Graham, A Sort of Life, Bodley Head, 1971.

Hine, Reginald, Hitchin Worthies, Dent, 1932.

Hine, Reginald, Lamb and His Hertfordshire, Dent.

Hopkinson, John, Francis Bacon, Hertfordshire Illustrated Review, 1894.

Houfe, Simon, Sir Albert Richardson: The Professor, White Crescent Press Ltd., Luton, 1980.

Jenkins, Elizabeth, Lady Caroline Lamb, Cardinal, 1974.

King, James, William Cowper. A Biography, Duke University Press, Durham, USA, 1986.

Kitton, F.C., Charles Dickens and Hertfordshire, Hertfordshire Constitutional Magazine, 1889.

Lamb, Charles, The Essays and Last Essays of Elia, Walter Scott Ltd., 1890.

Lamb Charles and Mary, The Letters. Edited by E. W. Marrs, Cornell University Press, New York, 1975/8.

Lytton, Earl of, The Life of Edward Bulwer, First Lord Lytton, MacMillan, 1913.

MacFarlane, Constance, The Life of Robert Bloomfield, Wm. Carling & Co., Hitchin, 1916.

MacLean, Catherine MacDonald, Mark Rutherford. A Biography of William Hale White, MacDonald, 1955.

Munro, Ian S., Leslie Mitchell: Lewis Grassic Gibbon, Oliver & Boyd, Edinburgh, 1966.

Osborne, Dorothy, The Letters, Edited by Judge Parry, 1888.

Oxford Companion to English Literature, 5th Edition, Edited by Margaret Drabble, OUP, 1985.

Oxford Literary Guide to the British Isles, Edited by Dorothy Eagle and Hilary Carnell, OUP. 1977.

Pepys, Samuel, The Diary, in 3 Vols., Edited by John Warrington, Dent, 1953.

Potter, Beatrix, The Journals 1881–1897, Transcribed by Leslie Linder, Frederick Warne, 1966.

Pound, Reginald, Arnold Bennett, William Heinemann Ltd., 1952.

Prouty, C. T., George Gascoigne, Columbia University Press, New York, 1942.

Rinder, Frank, George Chapman: Poet and Dramatist, Hertfordshire Illustrated Review, 1894.

Robert, Rudolph, Famous Authors in Hertfordshire, Hertfordshire Countryside/Letchworth Printers Ltd., 1970.

Sherry, Norman, The Life of Graham Greene, Vol. 1, (1904–1939), Jonathan Cape, 1989.

Snow, C. P., Trollope, MacMillan, 1975.

Southwood, Martin, John Howard, Independent Press Ltd., 1958.

Stansky, Peter, & Abrahams, William, Orwell: The Transformation, Constable & Co. Ltd., 1979.

Thomas, Edward, A Literary Pilgrim in England, OUP, 1980 Edition.

Trollope, Anthony, An Autobiography, World's Classics
  Edition, 1961.

White, William Hale, The Early Life of Mark Rutherford,
  Humphrey Milford/OUP, 1913.

Wickett, William, & Duval, Nicholas, The Farmer's Boy,
  Terence Dalton Ltd., Lavenham, 1971.

Wright, Thomas, The Life of Colonel Fred Burnaby,
  Everett & Co., 1908.

Ziegler, Philip, Melbourne,
  Collins, 1976.

# Index
## of People and Places

# Books Published by
# THE BOOK CASTLE

**JOURNEYS INTO HERTFORDSHIRE**: Anthony Mackay. Foreword by The Marquess of Salisbury, Hatfield House. Nearly 200 superbly detailed ink drawings depict the towns, buildings and landscape of this still predominantly rural county.

**JOURNEYS INTO BEDFORDSHIRE**: Anthony Mackay. Foreword by The Marquess of Tavistock, Woburn Abbey. A lavish book of over 150 evocative ink drawings.

**NORTH CHILTERNS CAMERA, 1863–1954: FROM THE THURSTON COLLECTION IN LUTON MUSEUM**: edited by Stephen Bunker. Rural landscapes, town views, studio pictures and unique royal portraits by the area's leading early photographer.

**LEAFING THROUGH LITERATURE: WRITERS' LIVES IN HERTFORDSHIRE AND BEDFORDSHIRE**: David Carroll. Illustrated short biographies of many famous authors and their connections with these counties.

**THROUGH VISITORS' EYES: A BEDFORDSHIRE ANTHOLOGY**: edited by Simon Houfe. Impressions of the county by famous visitors over the last four centuries, thematically arranged and illustrated with line drawings.

**FOLK: CHARACTERS and EVENTS in the HISTORY of BEDFORDSHIRE and NORTHAMPTONSHIRE**: Vivienne Evans. Arranged by village/town, an anthology of stories about the counties' most intriguing historical figures.

**ECHOES: TALES and LEGENDS of BEDFORDSHIRE and HERTFORDSHIRE**: Vic Lea. Thirty, compulsively retold historical incidents.

**JOHN BUNYAN: HIS LIFE and TIMES**: Vivienne Evans. Foreword by the Bishop of Bedford. Bedfordshire's most famous son set in his seventeenth century context.

**LOCAL WALKS: SOUTH BEDFORDSHIRE and NORTH CHILTERNS**: Vaughan Basham. Twenty-seven thematic circular walks.

**CHILTERN WALKS: BUCKINGHAMSHIRE**: Nick Moon. In association with the Chiltern Society, the first of a series of three guides to the whole Chilterns. Thirty circular walks.

**CHILTERN WALKS: OXFORDSHIRE and WEST BUCKINGHAMSHIRE**: Nick Moon. In association with the Chiltern Society, the second book of thirty circular walks.

**COUNTRY AIR: SUMMER and AUTUMN**: Ron Wilson. The Radio Northampton presenter looks month by month at the countryside's wildlife, customs and lore.

**WHIPSNADE WILD ANIMAL PARK: 'MY AFRICA'**: Lucy Pendar. Foreword by Andrew Forbes. Introduction by Gerald Durrell. Inside story of sixty years of the Park's animals and people – full of anecdotes, photographs and drawings.

**FARM OF MY CHILDHOOD, 1925–1947**: Mary Roberts. An almost vanished lifestyle on a remote farm near Flitwick.

**A LASTING IMPRESSION**: Michael Dundrow. An East End boy's wartime experiences as an evacuee on a Chilterns farm at Totternhoe.

**EVA'S STORY: CHESHAM SINCE the TURN of the CENTURY**: Eva Rance. The ever-changing twentieth-century, especially the early years at her parents' general stores, Tebby's, in the High Street.

**DUNSTABLE DECADE: THE EIGHTIES: – A Collection of Photographs**: Pat Lovering. A souvenir book of nearly 300 pictures of people and events in the 1980s.

**DUNSTABLE IN DETAIL**: Nigel Benson. A hundred of the town's buildings and features, plus town trail map.

**OLD DUNSTABLE**: Bill Twaddle. A new edition of this collection of early photographs.

**BOURNE AND BRED: A DUNSTABLE BOYHOOD BETWEEN THE WARS**: Colin Bourne. An elegantly written, well-illustrated book capturing the spirit of the town over fifty years ago.

**ROYAL HOUGHTON**: Pat Lovering. Illustrated history of Houghton Regis from the earliest times to the present.

## Specially for Children

**ADVENTURE ON THE KNOLLS: A STORY OF IRON AGE BRITAIN**: Michael Dundrow. Excitement on Totternhoe Knolls as ten-year-old John finds himself back in those dangerous times, confronting Julius Caesar and his army.

**THE RAVENS: ONE BOY AGAINST THE MIGHT OF ROME**: James Dyer. On the Barton hills and in the south-east of England as the men of the great fort of Ravensburgh (near Hexton) confront the invaders.

**Further titles are in preparation.**
**All the above are available via any bookshop, or from the**
**publisher and bookseller**
**THE BOOK CASTLE**
**12 Church Street, Dunstable, Bedfordshire, LU5 4RU**
**Tel: (0582) 605670**